D0923522

BEYOND
THE CHARTS

BEYOND
THE CHARTS

mp3 and the digital music revolution

BRUCE HARING

An OTC Press Book
Published by JM Northern Media LLC

An OTC Press Book
Published by JM Northern Media LLC
Queries regarding rights and permissions
should be addressed to our editorial offices
6363 Sunset Boulevard, 7th Floor, Los Angeles, CA 90028

Library of Congress Card Number
99-091636

ISBN No. 0-9674517-0-1

To my mother, Ann Haring,
whose faith and insight into
human nature saved my music career.

Contents

Author's Note

The inevitable query posed to an author upon delivery of a book is usually the last letter of the fabled "five W" questions of journalism – who, what, when, where, and why.

Why, indeed, would someone lock the door to the writing room for months on end, sustained only by Pink Dot and pages upon pages of meandering conversation transcripts, dusty newspapers, and musty magazine clippings?

In this case, the "why" was my need to explain the forces that were shaping the future of music, the most important messenger in popular culture.

Tightly-controlled radio playlists, the lack of focus in video, and the increasingly homogenous and profit-before-development stances of the major record companies – multinational corporations that largely determine which voices will be heard in the larger domains of the media – make the Internet's unprecedented opportunity for musicians to reach an audience even more urgent and necessary.

The rise of the Net as an alternative distribution channel has not escaped the notice of those currently at the top of the music food chain, even as they publicly dismiss it.

A subtle shift has emerged in their media strategy over the course of the last two years. Instead of confrontation and chest-thumping pronouncements on the danger to social order posed by the Internet, a gentler approach has been gradually instituted.

Now, the huge up-front money and promotional expertise of the establishment is being touted as beneficial to musicians. Of course, the touters of those services quietly add, contractual terms may have to be slightly altered to accommodate the new world order.

Their quid pro quo for a kinder, gentler contract will be a surrender of such formerly exclusive and untouchable rights as an artist's very name and image, locked up for eternity in exchange for a brief shot at the brass ring of stardom, a level attained by only a small percentage of acts in the history of recorded music.

Essentially, the deal amounts to a few dollars advanced by the company store before payday. In return, the workers of the industry – the musicians – are giving up any chance at making a living. Instead, they get the slim chance of making a killing. In the real world, that's called gambling.

It is my hope that this book ignites a better understanding and appreciation for the dangers and the opportunities that are possible during the coming years of the digital music revolution.

Let the battle continue.

Bruce Haring
November, 1999

Acknowledgments

It's never easy to pull a major project together, and this book and its accompanying web site certainly wouldn't have been born without the contributions and encouragement of numerous individuals.

I'd like to particularly thank those who took time out of their extremely busy schedules for interviews, fact-checks, and background conversations. Although we may not agree on every point, I salute their courage to address the issues shaping the emerging digital music world.

Special thanks to Larissa Le, one of the pioneers of the online world, who was present at the birth of this project and served as its inspiration. Without her professional expertise and guidance, it would not have been possible.

The infrastructure behind this book and its accompanying web site (www.OFFtheCHARTS.com) required a great deal of professional assistance.

Attorney Pamela Koslyn provided the legal direction on countless real world and cyberspace issues, as well as the support only good friends can give. Both were much appreciated.

Armando Llenado was the designer whose vision made the web site spring to life. His good humor in the face of countless changes made a complicated process easier. Thanks also to Howard Horowitz, whose sophisticated design work resulted in the book cover and jacket design.

Dawn Laureen supplied much of the photography that adorns this book. Her extraordinary effort to capture the nuances of the professionally harried characters of this narrative went beyond the call of duty, and is greatly appreciated. Tess Taylor, president of the National Association of Record Industry Professionals (NARIP) also supplied some hard-to-get photos, for which I am extremely grateful.

As always, Cathy Davis proved to be a great friend and problem-solver on issues and circumstances too numerous to detail. I can never thank her enough for her efforts.

Thanks also to Jolyn Matsumuro, who coordinated several activities on short notice despite the pressures of her own thriving public relations business, and Crystal Shepeard and Liz Redwing, whose transcriptions laid the foundation for the book.

Gratitude goes out to Nick Rubenstein and Jodi Wille of Dilettante Press, one of the leaders of the independent book publishing scene thriving in Silver Lake, for sharing their experience with me.

Much respect to Chuck D and John Perry Barlow for granting me permission to share their special insights with my audience.

Many friends, colleagues and coworkers provided advice, a sounding board, or just a friendly voice throughout the long hours of putting this project to bed. Grateful thanks to Jennifer Ballantyne, Anita Rivas, Maria Armoudian, Tim and Nancy Ryan, Richard Martini, Cary

ACKNOWLEDGMENTS

Baker, Bob Bernstein, Ami Kay Spishock, Tracey Miller, Diane and Phil Cornell, Camille Alcasid, Al Stewart, Terry Moseley, Tom Fox, Jill Richmond, Edna Gundersen, Bruce Schwartz, Melinda Newman, Hanna Bolte and Eileen Thompson for all your support.

My gratitude to Susan Martin and the staff at Omni Color.

Foreword

I think this is a fantastic time. I think this is an incredible time.

Right now, we're all going into this bold new world with our hands out in a dark room. The lawyers don't really know how to call it. They don't really know what to say.

What you're looking at is a mass splintering of the marketplace.

You want to talk about record companies screaming? With 300k broadband, a lot of people are going to scream, if they're not screaming now. Radio stations, TV stations, cable.

But record companies are the first wave to feel the pain.

And I can't say I feel all that sorry for them.

Number one, the industry has always depended on the naivete of the artist and the public. Simple equation: if you make the artist as naive as possible about the process, and you make the public as naive as possible about the process, you can always stake a claim to the importance of your need to be there in the first place.

In the past, it all had to go through that strainer. They had the distribution outlets, they determined the price of the product, they told you the amount of time you have to get a piece of product to the public, and they told you the minimum amount of sides that had to be delivered.

No more.

The Internet makes it possible to get the art from the artist to the public with as few middlemen as possible. For the first time, musicians are able to have an artist-to-world contact point.

I'm able to cut, put it up one night, and then that same night, somebody from New Zealand could check it out. That's unheard of in the past. With this possibility, you're seeing Stax Records all over again. Cut one week, up the next week.

I foresee by 2002 at least a million artists doing it on this alternative means to the traditional way of hoping that a major record company picks you up. The Internet offers a way that they can step onto the field and at least play minor league ball, and if the majors want to consider themselves major, then they have a fantastic recruiting ground to look at.

There's still some traps. I think in the future you'll have a two-pronged process – online contracts and off-line contracts. And I think people have to be wise enough to say they'll have an online situation and if a major wants to come get 'em, they got to buy two entities out.

My advice: you have to know what you have. Know the process that you're dealing with. It's almost going to be like surfboarding. You're going to surfboard through the waves, and there's sharks in the water, so make sure you know how to surf. You still have to know Music Business 101 to know what to duck and what to do.

This new world will serve as an alternative to the

many artists that either have been through the strainer and are finally savvy, and new artists that feel that they want to have a chance to get in the music business now, instead of shipping their DATs to L.A., New York, Nashville, London or wherever.

I truly believe that the old way will have to adapt to the new way. And it's hard for the new way to fit into an old template, so there's going to be some pain.

It's almost like baseball was the original, traditional American pastime. Football came along to a smaller crowd at first, but it was played on the same field, in many instances, and in the same stadiums, and grew to where it's now more popular.

Here you've got the same situation. The traditional record companies are baseball. Digital music is football. And the football crowds are getting bigger........

Chuck D
October 24, 1999

BEYOND THE CHARTS

ONE

Michael's Minute

Michael Robertson was driving along the 5 free-way North outside San Diego, balancing a cell phone against his ear and battling frequent drop-outs in his conversation.

It was an exhilarating night for Robertson, so the technical glitches couldn't spoil his upbeat mood. He had just celebrated one of the best moments of his life and was still energized as he headed to his house in the San Diego foothills.

That day, less than nine months after starting his digital music company, MP3.com, the 33-year old Robertson had closed his first major round of financing, a deal bringing $11 million into his operation.

To celebrate, he and 15 fellow employees gathered at a local restaurant to share a few laughs, a few drinks, some toasts and good food, the spoils of a battle they had been waging over nine months against some of the world's largest corporations.

Robertson's business was harvesting the potential of an audio compression format known as Moving Picture Experts Group-1 Layer 3, nicknamed MP3 by its users.

Developed in the early 1990s, MP3 squeezed a digital sound file down to a size practical for Internet distribution. Instead of spending hours downloading a song from the Net using other formats, MP3 made it possible for the average computer user to grab a song in minutes, while those with high-speed connections could obtain music in seconds.

Robertson didn't invent the format, but he was among the first to realize its potential to forever change the way music was distributed, marketed, and promoted.

In a world where few artists were treated well by big record companies, where MTV and radio had extremely narrow playlists, and a generation of music lovers was growing up with the Internet as part of their lives, MP3 offered a new way to connect music to the masses.

That ability worried the established order of the music industry, particularly since every compact disc on the market was a digital product that contained no security measures that would prevent it from being endlessly duplicated in the MP3 format and passed around the Internet.

At least, that was the public worry of the establishment.

Copyright infringement had been the bogeyman of the recording industry since home taping first reared its head in the 1950s. Now, the rise of the commercial Internet exponentially eased illegal distribution of copyrighted recordings, industry representatives claimed.

Evoking images of marauding buccaneers, the establishment railed against "pirates" who would unlawfully "rip," or encode, sound recordings and give away the booty to the world, thereby depriving the recording artists, songwriters, music publishers, and particularly record companies of their rightful compensation for transactions involving their intellectual property.

The theory sounded legitimate. But many observers, even those who worked closely with the recording industry, weren't buying it.

"I worked at a big record company and a pretty successful one, and I can tell you without hesitation we never spent one breath talking about piracy," said Steve Rennie, a former Epic Records executive and artist manager who switched to the Internet side when he joined ARTISTdirect, a company involved in e-commerce sites for bands. "This is a whole thing that's been concocted."

Rennie, echoing a theory best illustrated by the success of bands like the Grateful Dead, Black Crowes, Phish and others that permitted taping at their live shows, insisted that the greatest risk was not that music was going to be stolen.

"The greater risk is that your music is never going to be heard," Rennie said. "And the fact of the matter is record companies have been giving away music for years with the hope that they can introduce you to something that you might find value in and go out and buy it. So this whole thing about oh, my god, we're worried about protecting the rights of artists from piracy, frankly, is the big lie of what's going on."

Others were even more cynical than Rennie. "What MP3 has done for the music industry is give the devil a name," said musician Thomas Dolby Robertson (no relation to Michael Robertson), speaking to Rolling Stone magazine.

Privately, executives from big record companies agreed with Dolby.

While the copyrighted recordings under their control were at risk to digital distribution via the Internet, the executives also realized that large-scale piracy had bedeviled the industry since at least the 1960s. The potentially greater threat was the possibility that musicians would bypass the established distribution systems and deal directly with the marketplace.

MP3 became widespread by 1996 and quickly took hold among active music fans, particularly those on college campuses with ultra-fast Internet connections, becoming more popular than "sex" as an Internet search engine subject and the de facto digital music standard for files.

The recording industry was taken by surprise. They had envisioned a quieter, gentler transition away from physical goods, one that would be as tightly controlled and manipulated as the transition from vinyl albums to compact discs in the 1980s.

Because they were outspoken about MP3's ability to circumvent the existing system, and because they were not adverse to pointing out the entrenched music industry's flaws, Michael Robertson and his colleagues in the digital music realm were considered anarchists.

With no regard for the way things had always been done, fresh ideas borne of an outsider's naivete, and utterly fearless when it came to speaking truth to power, MP3.com quickly became the voice of the disenfranchised and the conscience of a music industry that had built its empire on the bones of musicians largely cheated of their rightful compensation.

Industry trade magazine Hits put it best about MP3.com's attitude: they "came screeching into the game, middle finger fully extended."

Robertson and other digital music pioneers heralded a new order. The world that for years turned a blind eye to record companies' compensating musicians with fleeting fame, old cars, and loans euphemistically referred to as "advances" was rapidly shifting.

Digital distribution had arrived, allowing popular songs to be morphed into codes that could easily be sent at the click of a mouse to computers anywhere in the world.

From a universe where warehouses, radio promotion and retail marketing money largely determined which songs would be exposed to the public, the Internet's mainstreaming to the consumer created one where, at least theoretically, anyone, anywhere, at any time, could share music with like-minded citizens.

"The question really is how will the record industry survive?" asked Thomas Dolby Robertson, speaking at the Digital Distribution and the Music Industry '99 conference in Los Angeles. "In effect, they've had an unfair advantage over everybody else for the last few decades, and that unfair advantage is very clearly threatened and undermined by what is effectively a much more efficient way of getting music from the musician to the fan."

*   *   *

Since the creation of the printing press forever democratized intellectual property, technology has always challenged the status of copyright holders with new means of reproduction and distribution.

But never were they so threatened than by the mainstream acceptance of the Internet, the first mass market tool for electronic transmission of intellectual property beyond a regional audience.

The idea of such widespread freedom scared the old guard. Much as Samuel Johnson referred to patriotism as the last refuge of a scoundrel, so did many in the music industry couch their Internet agenda by hoisting a banner for the plight of the artist, the same body whose labors they had for years egregiously exploited.

Copyrights must be protected, record executives and their associates shouted to all who would listen. The artists deserve to be compensated for their works. And surely, they argued, the record company has a valuable trove of intellectual property that also deserves the same protection and considerations.

Such pleas found resonance among some fans and mainstream media, many of them blind to the financial arrangements of the music industry and its checkered history of such accounting and contractual esoterica as free goods, breakage, and packaging deductions, most of them poison to the artist bottom line, some of them outdated by 10 to 15 years.

Even more pernicious, the digital music age brought new proposals to impose deductions on musicians' royalties onto the table, proposals that went beyond taking money for manufacturing and promotion and extending into such areas as ticketing, merchandising, and requests for Internet domain names.

In the 1990s, most acts made little if anything on recording royalties, relying on huge advances that were recoupable through a variety of strange accounting methods. The result was that most recording acts were required to sell a half-million records to approach the break-even point, making most of their money from live performances, merchandise sales, and, if a songwriter, performance fees garnered from radio and television broadcasters.

Veteran entertainment industry attorney Jay Cooper explained the recording company contractual subterfuge at a seminar in Santa Monica, Calif. in early 1999.

The typical recording artist contract that promises to pay 14 percent of a CD's $16.98 retail price usually delivers substantially less, Cooper said.

"They have all types of clauses in the hundred page (contracts) that tell you why they pay you something less than that," Cooper said.

"Some companies deduct 10% for "breakage," he said. "There is no such thing as breakage. They deduct 25% for packaging, about $4.00, and packaging costs about 35 cents. They deduct another 15% for what they call free goods. There are no "free" records. They sometimes deduct another 25% for CDs because they say they're still developing CDs, so they should pay less for CDs."

In the end, Cooper said, "they make all these deductions and what you come out with is a royalty that is equivalent to about half of what 14% is of $16.98."

Record companies had always asked their artists for royalty relief whenever new formats or marketing concepts were introduced. Compact discs sold were paid at vinyl rates for some artists; and the introduction of the Sony MiniDisc and Philips' Digital Compact Cassette brought requests for 30% royalty breaks.

With digital distribution, a format where manufacturing and distribution costs were eliminated, record companies were contemplating asking for a provision that would subtract up to 25% of the royalty rate owed on a record for Internet promotion, a term which had not even been defined, much less implemented, at large record companies.

*   *   *

But in the digital age, a new breed of entrepreneur was rising, one that didn't have to rely on relationships with the old school or contractual flim-flam in order to achieve its means.

The new entrepreneurs came from the computer industry, which had long before dealt with its own hue and cry over copyright issues. The computer industry had quickly learned that encryption was merely a barrier to more widespread use of its products, and quickly discarded the notion that protections could be designed that would forever safeguard software. It proved to be a wise decision, one that led to a flourishing industry.

Record companies were slow to recognize the perils to their business spawned by the rise of the Internet. As late as 1998, many companies did not have staff whose job was to monitor activities on the Net. Most senior executives, when they paid attention at all, dismissed the Net as just another passing fad, the CB radio of the 1990s. Many executives privately felt that any changes that did develop would happen long after they were safely retired.

As such, the entrenched executives felt that supporting a new philosophy of distributing music, one which embraced a direct relationship with the consumer, was something that needed to be avoided at all costs. Their attitude amounted to a stone wall: we work for companies that have multinational reach and resources. We have the relationships. And more to the point, we have the artists under contract. We control the system. There is no need to change.

Such arrogance was not unlike that seen in numerous movie villains, whose undoing is inevitably wrought by their hubris at the expense of the smaller and weaker.

Enter Michael Robertson, a lean young San Diego entrepreneur who hardly listened to music, but recognized its value on the Internet.

It was almost as if Robertson was a character in some old Western movie, riding into Dodge and vowing to clean up the action from the corrupt sheriffs. Blonde, steely-eyed, straightforward, Robertson was the voice of the disenfranchised, one of the first music entrepreneurs who dared break the united front that the allegedly independent major record distributors in the United States erected against digital distribution.

For that, he would pay. At virtually every conference, Robertson was gang-attacked by the establishment, derided as naive or hopelessly out of touch. His answer was akin to the approach used in the Watergate hearings to great effect by North Carolina senator Sam Ervin, whose repeated mantra of "I'm just an old country lawyer" inevitably swayed his audience.

Admitting his naivete, Robertson would inevitably win over his audience by pointing out the logic of his position versus the record industry's established way of doing business. It was an approach that found great favor among the audiences of up-and-coming musicians, most of them dissatisfied by the barriers they faced in trying to get their music heard above the major label din.

But Robertson posed a danger beyond the fact that his company was challenging the established music order. In fact, if he were to succeed, his way of doing business could change the face of virtually every aspect of the entertainment industry, threatening rich and entrenched business interests across the globe.

To understand his challenge, it's instructive to look at the state of the music industry in the 1990s.

*   *   *

By the mid-1990s, the record industry had become the province of six multinational record distributors, all but one of them based outside the United States. Together, through direct ownership, licensing, distribution arrangements and other affiliations, they controlled well over 90% of the music market in the U.S., and an equally huge share outside that territory.

But such dominance was both blessing and curse. While steady streams of cash flow brightened the bottom lines and made stockholders happy, it came at a price. Over-expansion fueled by the advent of the compact disc and the subsequent replacement of vinyl record collections had made the infrastructures dangerously oversized.

Thus, when consumers had eventually replaced their collections, a downturn in worldwide music sales in the mid-1990s was causing alarm bells to sound at record company headquarters, which required quarterly earnings to constantly improve, a theme familiar to Wall Street.

To do that, most record companies had come to rely on a scatter-shot approach to talent scouting. Sign as many bands as possible, and then let an ugly rugby scrum ensue. The one or two winners that rose to the top would make up for the losers.

The problem with that scenario was the cultural genocide that was its by-product. Bands were signed at very early stages of their career, and cast quickly aside if they did not produce the requisite massive sales with the first or second album. It was a practice borne of economics, where commerce ruled instead of art.

If such tactics were applied at the dawn of the record industry, many prominent artists whose successes came after several albums would have suffered. Would Bruce Springsteen have survived the tepid sales of "Greetings from Asbury Park?" Would Bob Dylan, the voice of a generation but never a huge record seller, have been dropped?

Although many, if not most, executives in the record industry paid lip service to the concept of artist development, few were willing to risk their positions at the multinationals to challenge the way business was done for any extended period.

Thus, the industry became a self-perpetuating cycle of rises and falls, as acts across the music spectrum quickly flared and then spent their wad. Arrested Development, Wilson Phillips, Veruca Salt, Poi Dog Pondering, Jen Trynin, all highly-touted, most gone in a flash.

By 1998, the record industry had hit a lull in sales and a new low in style. Relying on teenage pop stars, soundtracks, and stars from two decades ago, it had seemingly reached a cultural and economic saturation point.

SoundScan, a data information system which tracks point-of-purchase sales of recorded music product at key stores and then extrapolates a number to represent the actual sales (much as political polling projects election winners based on surveys of a relative handful of voters), issued a top ten report on the best-selling albums for 1998.

Topping the list was the soundtrack to "Titanic," which far-outdistanced its competition by moving 9,338,061 units. Trailing was "Let's Talk About Love," a Celine Dion album moving 5,859,421 units.

The list doesn't get any more cutting edge from

there. Backstreet Boys, Shania Twain, 'N Sync, Garth Brooks, Will Smith, Savage Garden, and the soundtracks to the films "City Of Angels" and "Armageddon" rounded out the list. None would ever be considered groundbreaking.

Boosted by "Titanic," one of the best-selling albums in years, the industry still couldn't muster much of an overall increase in CD shipments (which could still be returned), moving 847 million units, up from 1997's 753.1 million, according to figures amassed by the Recording Industry Association of America, the leading trade organization.

At the same time, the massive wealth of Wall Street generated by the longest economic boom in U.S. history was having a profound effect on the music landscape.

Ignoring stagnant CD sales figures, a wave of bankruptcies at retail, and the increased costs of promotion and marketing, Wall Street players funded several startup record company ventures. However, those ventures launched by the mid-1990s were mostly run by elder statesmen from the record industry, back for yet another try at a gold record.

Richard Branson, founder of Virgin Records, found some investors to buy into his charisma and fund the cheekily named V2 Records. Walter Yetnikoff, the former CBS Records head who brokered that company's deal to Sony before being ousted by his own habits and lieutenants, returned from exile with VelVel Records; and ex-MCA Music chief Al Teller rejoined the party with his own Red Ant Records.

"Although the industry's a bit flat at the moment, it's still a massive industry," explained Branson as he prepared for the rollout of V2's first albums. "And it's still a massively profitable industry. I mean, if you went to any of the parties after the Grammys, every single person seemed to get a full bowl of caviar and Dom Perignon champagne."

Branson had sold Virgin to fellow Britishers Thorn EMI in 1992 for just shy of a billion dollars, the biggest price ever paid for a record label. Four years later, the agreement not to compete with his former company had ended, allowing the daredevil balloonist to come back to a business that thrives on hot air.

Some old music business friends were glad to have him.

"Quite a lot of artists working with the majors were saying, "We miss the independent feel that Virgin had," Branson says. "They say, "We're just one of 600 artists in this big company." Sadly, if you're that big, you become quite impersonal."

V2's charter pointedly noted that it would avoid the "them and us" mentality which has led to a rash of litigation between major record companies and "prominent artists," code words for Prince, George Michael and Don Henley, all of whom had challenged the business practices of their labels with high-profile litigation.

At Red Ant (Ant being an acronym for Alvin N. Teller), CEO Teller, who would later segue to his own Internet venture, Atomic Pop, agreed with Branson that the business model of big record labels no longer fit.

"It's just become an unwieldy one," Teller said. "It just doesn't work. The radio marketplace is completely fragmentated. The whole notion of marketing really is very different than it used to be. It's very difficult for large, sort of monolithic label structures to handle that for a large number of releases."

But it was also a whole lot of fun to run a record label, as both Branson and Teller readily admitted.

In fact, Yetnikoff, the one time bad boy of rock 'n roll whose days of drinking, snorting and carousing at Sony were the stuff of industry legend, said fun was the main reason he got back in the game.

Although admittedly reformed from the days when he claimed he would worry about a packet of cocaine falling out of his pocket during business meetings with Sony executives, Yetnikoff still had a mischievous streak.

"All these heads of companies seem so sour," Yetnikoff lamented during his VelVel launch. "I don't want to go through names, but some are sort of fat, though not in all cases; some are bald, not in all cases; and sour, in all cases. I would like to have some levity. People say the business is yuck. They want I should make it un-yuck."

Yetnikoff's efforts aside, something was on the horizon that offered blessed relief from the traditional record industry.

*　　　　　　　*　　　　　　　*

At the same moment as the record industry's decline, a new medium had captured the attention of the public. The Internet, long the province of scientists and academics, had blossomed into a commercial platform.

The history of the Internet is a tale of conflicting perceptions, most of them having to do with who deserves credit for which facet of its development.

From Oct. 29, 1969, when the first node of the computer network known as the Arpanet was connected between the laboratory of UCLA professor Leonard Kleinrock and Stanford University, dreamers had envisioned a world where planet-wide communication and video conferencing was possible.

But the system Kleinrock and his associates first tapped into was a network that couldn't be reached by any computer anywhere on the planet. That changed in 1973, when scientists Vint Cerf and Robert Kahn defined the Internet protocol that allowed packets of information to be sent from any computer to any other computer. Their research took until 1983, when the system that today is recognized as the Internet actually rolled out.

The next big leap forward for the online world was

the invention by Tim Berners-Lee of the World Wide Web. Berners-Lee came up with the software standards that created a global hypertext links system which enabled easy transmission of graphics and access to any computer with just a few easily-mastered commands.

In the early 1990s, the arrival of the Mosaic browser, developed at the University of Illinois by the team that would later found Netscape, heralded the birth of the commercial age of the World Wide Web. Mosaic, the first easy to install and use browser, made graphic images viewable.

While the music industry was aware of the Net, computers were still largely perceived as the province of academics, the military, scientists and serious geeks.

That, in part, explains why the fast-living entertainment industry paid only scant attention to its rise. That was the opening for a new breed of entrepreneur eager to fill a niche.

*   *   *

Michael Robertson grew up in and around Los Angeles county, going to high school at Westminster High in a middle class area of Huntington Beach, California, a town immortalized as "Surf City" by the Beach Boys.

Despite the bucolic Southern California setting, dominated by surfers and defense workers, it was not the typical family.

"Well, normal for the '90s, maybe," said Robertson. "Broken family, alcoholic... traditional sob story. I had a single mom, four kids to raise, no job skills."

Robertson stuck close to home for his college choice, matriculating at the University of California at San Diego.

"I started off in political science," recalled Robertson. "But I got pretty disillusioned with an extraordinarily left-leaning staff at UC San Diego and said, "I can't take this."

Robertson was a self-admitted decent student, "not a spectacular student or anything like that. I averaged

3.0." But his analytical side was attracted to a discipline known as cognitive science, the study of intelligence.

"You can think of it as figuring out how the brain works," he said. The study encompasses neurobiology, psychology, and human-computer interface design.

The ultimate premise of cognitive science is figuring out how you design something so that people can interact with it in an easy way, a skill that would serve him well.

"That's what attracted me to it," says Robertson. "I really liked the technology part, but I didn't just want to be a coding machine, taking four years of how to program. I wanted to expand the horizon a little bit."

Robertson's independent side was evident early, as he worked his way through college. His glamourous jobs included stints at a copy center revising resumes, game room recreation monitor, and coach of the UC San Diego cycling team.

Eventually, Robertson found his way to the Supercomputer Center, "really where I grew up in a lot of ways," he said. "Clearly, from a technical standpoint. Because, as everyone knows, the Internet really thrived on the educational campuses to get going. Well, that's where I was living, that's where I worked. I was part of that."

As an undergrad, Robertson did research assistance, getting a broad exposure to technology. It would prove to be invaluable in Robertson's later career at MP3.com

But as it does for all students, graduation loomed, ripping away the veil of protection afforded by the campus life. Robertson eagerly embraced the opportunity.

"I've always been independent," he said. "It's probably never been my goal to go work for a company. I bucked up near graduation and I said, "Well, what am I going to do? I can always get a job as a programmer, but it seemed like, you know, I didn't really want that kind of a job."

After his 1990 graduation, a friend in the consulting

field convinced him to start his own consulting service for various hi-tech companies.

That led to a return to the San Diego Supercomputer Center. Robertson quickly sized up an opportunity.

"I needed some software that would do certain things, that would manage a network and do security audits and things like that. And so I wrote some software to do that." The effort later became a company, MR Mac Software.

But the proverbial light bulb was going off for Robertson.

"I did something which was pretty innovative then, it's like ridiculously obvious today," he said. "What I did back then is I made a software program where I put it out on the net and operated in a demo fashion. And what you could do is order it, and all you had to do is e-mail a credit card and I would e-mail you an activation code and that was it. It's a done deal. Nowadays, that's no big deal, but in 1992, that was a big deal. And, of course, I'm looking at this going, "Huh?" 95% margins? I think I can live with that."

The small niche company specialized in security auditing tools, but Robertson wanted something bigger with more mainstream potential. "So I started another company called Media Minds, which was a digital camera software company. We made software for digital cameras. The easiest way to describe it is that you could make a photo album on your computer."

It proved to be a disaster.

"We made a bet and we were wrong," said Robertson.

The company folded and Robertson lost a lot of money. Worse, it was mostly his own money, including a second mortgage on his house.

"I was disappointed. I had made the entrepreneurial bet. And I lost. But that's life."

Strangely enough, what was Robertson's ultimate failure didn't send him to bed for a week. Instead, he found it to be the ultimate motivation.

"I like challenges. Plain and simple. I like challenges," he said. "So if you want to motivate me, just tell me that you can't, you won't, you're not able to, and that motivates me. I was horribly disappointed (in the company), because I had invested a lot of time and money and thought it was a good idea. But I'm the kind of guy that doesn't look back too much, just keeps looking forward."

When he saw his company going downhill, Robertson began thinking what his next move would be.

"What we learned was listen to the consumer. Listen to that customer. You can have the best idea in the world, you can have the best engineers in the world, but if the customers aren't there, it doesn't matter."

From that sprang Robertson's next venture, the Z Company. "The model that I was enamored with was creating a service on the web, where you build this thing one time and it will work for one person or 10,000 or 10 million. The classic example is the search engine. You build it once and it operates the same with very little difference if one person uses it or 10 million."

The only problem: what would the Z Company do?

Software search engine Filez.com, designed to locate software updates on the web, and Websitez, a domain name search engine, were the first stabs. Both generated some online traffic, but their lack of a revenue stream outside advertising troubled Robertson.

However, the basic premise of both sites – serve the customer – still intrigued him. So Robertson began searching for other business opportunities using the same model.

It wasn't the best of times. Robertson was still working out of his home and recovering from the financial fallout of his previous venture.

"We were still in the macaroni and cheese era where you're looking for opportunity and you're watching your pennies and buying your equipment on credit cards so you get an extra 30 days to pay for it," Robertson recalled.

One of Robertson's hobbies was looking at Internet traffic charts, watching which sites were doing the most and the least visitors. At the same time, he had heard several mentions of MP3.

Robertson had a method of looking at the charts. "People always focus on the top. But if you're an entrepreneur, all the opportunity's at the bottom. You know, who's in 50,000th place that wasn't on the list last week, because that's where I can compete, cause it's the new opportunities."

He noticed several MP3 sites on the traffic list. "So I said, "well, I don't know what this MP3 thing is, but whatever it is, we should have one."

Robertson does not remember the title of the first MP3 file he downloaded.

But he was impressed with its results. "You know, to think, "I don't have a song, I click a button, boom! I have this great-sounding song." I was like, "Wow. This is pretty neat."

Robertson's enthusiasm was shared by an underground network of music enthusiasts. Standing in their way were six multinational corporations.

*   *   *

Hilary Rosen is president and chief executive officer of the Recording Industry Association of America, a Washington, D.C. trade group representing the U.S. sound recording industry. The RIAA's roster of more than 250 companies are responsible for creating, manufacturing, and/or distributing 90 percent of all sound recordings sold in the United States.

Rosen was a veteran Capitol Hill lobbyist, a founding board member of Rock the Vote, which encourages political participation among young people, and served on many non-profits. She was also a highly-vocal activist for free speech, winning the American Civil Liberties Union's Torch of Liberty Award.

Although Rosen was known for occasional flashes of temper – a reputation that served her well in dealing with her powerful and oft-arrogant constituents – she was well-suited to be the public face of the world's largest record companies in the United States, regarded as an articulate, intelligent and well-respected advocate.

But her job description also required Rosen to be the bad cop for U.S. recording company agendas, both public and private.

In the case of digital music, it was a role she took on with the zeal she had previously reserved for more liberal causes.

Unfortunately, the kind of lobbying and rational arguments that proved so successful with powerful legislators and other establishment figures would translate into a public relations nightmare when used on the Internet community that spawned the digital music movement. Instead of encouraging an early spirit of education and building support, the RIAA drove fans and musicians who already had a healthy dose of contempt for big recording companies further into the underground.

"It was the test case for whether the Internet could represent the de-institutionalization of America, that sort of sense of power to the people," Rosen said in 1999, reflecting back on the early years of digital music. "The Internet is going to mean we don't need rules, we don't need distribution, we don't need The Man, whoever The Man was. And music was sort of the first thing that gave people a taste of, "Well, does this work? Can we really get away without The Man?"

That issue is still in flux. But it could be argued that

the U.S. record companies, so concerned about the ramifications of change that many senior executives stalled the arrival of digital music, instead created a movement that flourished precisely because it managed to position itself as the angry alternative to the status quo.

But, as history shows, resisting technological change that would later provide new opportunities for growing its business was nothing new for the U.S. recording industry.

In The Beginning

By the mid 1980s, the street hustlers and promoters who made up the bulk of the early record industry executives had given way to a collective of multinational corporations.

Lured to the game by the "synergy" created when software and hardware companies came together, such giants as Philips Electronics, Sony Corp., Time Warner and Bertelsmann all made significant investments in the U.S. music industry, the main source of repertoire for worldwide music.

They entered a business with a long history of growth built on technology, and also one that had a long history of using copyrights as a speed bump to such growth.

"The Recording Industry Association of America has always advanced the agenda of the major labels in Washington through application of copyright laws while maintaining antitrust compliance," said its fellow traveler, the National Association of Recording Merchandisers, in a

1999 newsletter.

The music industry had an odd love/hate relationship with technology. While its growth had always depended on new formats and delivery systems spurring consumers to replace or expand their current music collections, the industry had also used a Chicken Little approach on each development.

Tape recorders, double-well drives for cassettes, digital audio tape, the compact disc – each had produced much hand-wringing, inevitably leading to intense lobbying for new, government-enforced protectionism for the U.S. recording industry.

As far back as the turn of the century, before the existence of a formal record industry, copyright battles over music were being fought.

The automatic music business, best exemplified by the player piano, was in full bloom, churning out scrolls that allowed machines to replay songs with little human assistance. Freed from the burden of learning an instrument, music lovers dived into the new medium, resulting in booming sales early in the 20th century.

There was just one problem. Piano roll companies did not want to pay for the right to reproduce the songs on their scrolls.

A suit was filed by music publishers, but the U.S. Supreme Court knocked them down, saying that copyrights would only protect songs that could be read by the human eye. Piano rolls were read by machine

Eventually, Congress was persuaded by the music interests to pass a law requiring companies that "mechanically" reproduced songs to pay a royalty to song publishers, a rule later applied to other sound recording mediums.

At the same time that player piano music was capturing the public fancy, another conveyance arrived on the scene. The 10-inch 78 record, named after its rotational speed of 78 revolutions per minute, debuted in 1901.

The 78 lasted until 1947, when it was supplanted by the LP (long-playing) stereophonic "hi-fi" record, whose superior sonic fidelity came forth when played at 33 1/3 RPM.

While tape recording cartridges were developed in 1930, followed by the first portable audiotape recorder in 1951 and stereo audiotapes on reels in 1956, tapes remained strictly a hobbyist phenomenon until 1958. That's when RCA introduced a 30-minute tape cartridge that sold for $1 more than a vinyl album.

While this price point helped, the cassette took some time to make an impact on the market, viewed as sonically inferior and less durable than the album by consumers, musicians and record companies, thus remaining an alternative, fringe medium.

Its commercial breakthrough came in 1964, when Philips introduced its own format for the tape cassette and allowed the specifications to be duplicated by other manufacturers. A new market was born, as inexpensive tape cassettes proved a nice and portable alternative to reel-to-reel tape.

But even without a huge commercial market for pre-recorded music in the format, the combination of cheap cassettes and portable recorders that could allow home taping at a reasonable fidelity caused concern in the record industry.

At the end of the 1960s, a blank tape cost roughly $3, compared to $6 for a vinyl album. The temptation was too great for savings in the collector's music budget, particularly in the flourishing counter-culture of the times.

In the early 1970s, executives from the recording industry began lamenting that blank cassette sales were impacting record sales. Teenagers were taping their favorite albums and swapping them among themselves, the executives complained.

The music industry was feeling heady. Thanks to complaints about vinyl bootlegging, the U.S. Congress had deemed sound recordings worthy of copyright protection in the 1971 Sound Recording Amendment to the 1909 Copyright Statute. Thus, there was reason to believe that a tariff on blank tape could be legislated.

But because sales of music continued to grow, and because the music industry was not at that time a truly effective Washington lobbying machine, the objections to home taping did not produce results.

At that point, the first pre-recorded products released solely on cassette began making their way into the commercial mix. Despite mostly esoteric experiments (the band Throbbing Gristle was a notable early adopter), the cassette began to gain some momentum

By the late '70s, the new wave, punk and disco booms had died, and the U.S. economy was stagnant, leading the record industry to a serious sales slump.

It was time to turn to the legislature for a solution.

An industry-wide effort led to an anti-home taping campaign that would be echoed when the age of electronic digital music dawned. Home taping was theft, the record industry argued. It's copyright infringement. They demanded a tax on blank tapes.

Congress yawned and did little, but the RIAA came back in the 1980s to protest dual-well cassette decks, which allowed duplication using one machine. Again, the record industry asked for a tax, this time on the decks as well.

In both cases, the recording industry made its artists – many of whom were still being paid royalties that amounted to pennies on the dollar by their record companies – the poster children behind their fight. The pleas did not resonate with Congress, perhaps because they noticed the boom that was occurring in a certain sector of music conveyances.

*   *   *

The music industry had long sought a conveyance that would improve sound and require less handling by consumers.

Several awkward and somewhat misguided attempts to improve on the limitations of the vinyl album arrived in the '70s. Neither quadraphonic sound, 8-track tapes or digital albums made any lasting impact among consumers, although truck drivers developed a fondness for the 8-track that didn't extend to the general population.

But the promise of something better was on the horizon: the compact disc, and its kissing cousin, digital audio tape.

While better audio quality and durability was the altruistic promise of the compact disc, which launched with a campaign touting "perfect sound forever," the sweet sound truly sought by the music industry was that of the old-fashioned cash register ring.

For once, they looked to technology for an answer.

The music industry financed its explosive growth in the 1980s by unilaterally declaring the death of the vinyl album in favor of the CD, resulting in the greatest boom period in audio recording history, albeit most of it created by re-selling the same music to the same people

Although digital technology had actually been around since the 1930s, when Bell Labs first dabbled in recorded sounds, NHK, Japan's broadcasting system, is generally credited with creating the first digital recordings, which were used for broadcasting and the station archives.

While Decca had experimented with digital sound in 1969, Sony is considered to have made the first commercial releases, a series of classical music audiophile albums issued in the early '70s by the Nippon/Columbia venture. It would soon be followed by other classical label digital products.

Philips Electronics of the Netherlands and Sony announced in 1978 that they were teaming up to develop the compact disc under a uniform standard. (In 1994, the Justice Department would investigate Sony Corp. and Philips Electronics for federal antitrust violations on the manufacturing and marketing of compact discs. Sony and Philips agreed in the 1970s to cross-license each others' patents on CD technology. But the Justice Department sent subpoenas to over a dozen companies to ask for details of their business relationships with Sony and Philips, seeking to find out whether licensing the technology violated federal anti-trust laws.)

The agreement to seek common ground did not mean that both companies had the same ideas. Sony favored a 12-inch format, while Philips, in turn, proposed a standard diameter of 12 centimeters. A Sony official later said that the 12-inch size, which could hold 13 hours of music, was chosen merely because it could contain the music to Beethoven's Ninth.

Philips and Sony also haggled over signal resolution. Philips voted for a 14-bit system, while Sony claimed the higher resolution of a 16-bit system was the answer.

Finally, in 1982, the war was over. The companies announced a worldwide standard that ensured that all compact discs could be played on all CD players, an agreement that covered such esoterica as sampling rates, optical wavelengths, error correction, size, and frequency response.

The first commercially released compact disc was issued in Japan on Oct. 1, 1982, Billy Joel's "52nd Street." Two years later, in September, 1984, Bruce Springsteen's "Born in the U.S.A." became, appropriately, the first CD manufactured in the United States.

But many record companies beyond Sony and PolyGram were hesitant to support the new format, recalling the time lag for the cassette to catch on and such disasters as the 8-track tape and quadraphonic sound.

The lack of copy protection also troubled manufacturers, who feared they would be issuing master discs that would last until the end of time to a world filled with pirates.

"The former chairman of Warner Bros. is on our board, and he said that they used to have wild arguments in the early '80s about whether they were going to do CDs or not," said Steve Devick, the CEO of Platinum Entertainment.

As history shows, the record industry woke up to what it would be missing out on, swallowed hard and took the plunge. But the CD wasn't the only concern when it came to fear of technology.

*   *   *

While the CD was just taking wing, the RIAA also sought yet another legislative answer to its perceived home taping problem.

In 1985, the U.S. House of Representatives considered the Home Audio Recording Act, which asked for a penny-per-minute tax on blank tape, a 10 percent tariff on the retail cost of tape recorders, and a whopping 25 percent tax on the retail cost of dual-well cassette decks.

The record companies, those peculiar institutions that treated their artists with benign neglect unless they were currently topping the charts, would receive the money from those taxes and distribute them to copyright owners.

A wacky clause in the bill exempted amateur musicians, home tapers recording their own collections, and others using tape recorders for their own use. No method of determining how individuals in the privacy of their own homes would be made to comply with that rule was suggested.

The House wisely knocked the Bill down. But the RIAA had not yet begun to fight.

Moving its offices to Washington, D.C. from New York in the late '80s, the trade organization regrouped and found a new target: digital audio tape, which eliminated much of the noise and hiss associated with reproductions using analog tapes.

Once again, Congress considered whether to vote in a record industry request for protection. This time, the recording industry lobbied for a bill that would force DAT manufacturers to add anti-copying locks to their devices. Although this measure didn't pass, Congress legislated royalty payments for the sale of DAT player and tapes.

But the failed effort on anti-copying safeguards didn't end efforts to obtain protections by audio interests. That obsession would later result in the Audio Home Recording Act of 1992, whose language would become a key battleground in the digital music age. Ironically, the very same forces who originally opposed laws governing digital recording devices – companies like Matsushita and Sony – now backed them. They had purchased record companies since their initial objections.

*   *   *

Sales of CD hardware were slow at first. Cassette players and turntables still ruled in all but audiophile households. Still, with plenty of money at stake, an industry coalition of hardware and software manufacturers known as the Compact Disc Group set to work to overcome objections. History records that it was not that hard a sell.

Overseas companies handled much of the early manufacturing, and capacity issues actually led labels to pick and choose which artists would be issued on CD first. Packaging issues also needed to be addressed. While the jewelbox, the hard, clam-shell outer casing for the CD, was readily accepted, retailers asked for something else to cover the somewhat crackable casing.

Eventually, the industry standard became the 6x12

cardboard container known as the longbox, a size chosen because two CDs would fit side by side in standard 12x12 record bins, eliminating the need for retailers to refixture their stores.

(Later in the decade, these arguments for the 6x12 would be tossed aside, as ecologically-minded opponents of the 6x12 rightly pointed out the wastefulness of the additional paperboard wrapper. After months of intense but fruitless negotiations between retailers and manufac- turers, and several attempts at developing earth-friendly alternative packaging, the record industry unilaterally ditched the longbox, offering a small rebate to retailers to ease the transition period).

Once the CD and its wrapping was standardized, the hard part started. Consumers needed to be prodded to rush the cash register for a product many neither wanted nor needed.

The biggest barrier was the high price of the hard- ware and software.

The first CD players were Sony's CDP-101, fol- lowed shortly by a Magnavox model, both retailing around $1,000. Because of the lack of domestic CD manu- facturing plants, the average retail price of the CD was $16 to $18, the high price in part justified by the need to import the product from Germany and Japan. Naturally, the high price kept the market isolated to what were termed "upscale audiophiles," with most early CDs issued in classical music.

In June, 1983, the first U.S. CD releases were issued, including a dozen titles from CBS, 30 from Denon, and 15 from Telarc. PolyGram followed in August with 100 CD titles, 80 of them classical music.

Jim Fifield, former president and CEO of EMI Music, explained the impact of the compact disc on the music industry during an interview in the mid 1990s.

"I've done an analysis which resulted in giving a

lot of presentations," said Fifield. "It was part of my learning curve about what were the biggest reasons why the music industry has grown over time.

The biggest factor in growth, explained Fifield, was technology. The cassette and the Walkman brought portability. "And then here comes the CD, which is of superior quality with instant access to tracks, and it's relatively indestructible in nature. That's why EMI has always been supportive of new technology. Because if any of those new technologies grab hold, the music industry is going to go through another big boom."

Unfortunately for the music industry, Fifield was gone from EMI by the time digital distribution became an issue the record industry needed to address.

*   *   *

Among the first digital sound files to make its mark on consumers was the .wav, developed by Microsoft and used for system sounds within Windows and other software programs. With no compression ratio, its sound quality was poor and .wav files took enormous time to download.

Also early on the scene were .au files, the Sun Microsystems proprietary sound format, usually used for Linux and UNIX systems. Like .wav files, they weren't really designed for downloading so much as performance within the computer system and on web pages.

Bulletin board systems were the main hub of early online music activity in .wav and .au files, providing hubs where fans willing to endure the long wait could swap songs. Because this very underground movement flew under the radar of the music industry – and because with the limited compressions, a three-minute song could take hours at the 2400 baud rate – little movement against these swaps was evident.

Compression technology developments changed that landscape. Compression works by eliminating redundancies in data and can work for any kind of file – text, programs, images, audio, video and virtual reality. Once transmitted, a decompression algorithm reverses the compression, allowing computer users access to the data.

With the personal computer boom, programmers began developing specific computer algorithms for data compression. The applications generally would read a file from the hard disc, compress the data, and save the file to the hard disc in a new format.

These "codecs," an acronym for coder/decoder, reduced the number of bytes in large files and programs without loss in quality.

There are numerous standard codecs. Some are used mainly to minimize file transfer time and are employed on the Internet. Others are intended to maximize the data that can be stored in a given amount of disk space or on a CD-ROM.

In the case of audio, codecs are generally measured by how close to the original music the transferred file sounds.

For music fans particularly concerned with that, something special was in development.

    *   *   *

In 1987, the same year DAT was introduced in Japan, the Moving Picture Experts Group, working under the supervision of the International Organization for Standardization in Geneva and the International Electro-Technical Commission, began researching and developing a way to compress digital video.

The organization was part of a joint European effort to devise standards for moving pictures and audio on the Internet.

After sometimes contentious battles between hardware, software and other interests, the results of the group's research arrived in 1992 as the MPEG format. Besides video, it could also reduce the storage space needed for a sound file without sacrificing quality.

MPEG offers three audio coding schemes, called Layer 1, Layer 2, and Layer 3, with the sound quality improving from Layer 1 to Layer 3.

There are numerous standard codec schemes. Some are used mainly to minimize file transfer time. Others allow more data to be stored on a disc.

MPEG-1 Layer 3 was described by its inventors as a perceptual audio coding scheme, meaning it exploited the properties of the human ear in trying to maintain the original sound quality of whatever file was being compressed.

The audio coding of MPEG-1 Layer 3 shrunk data by a factor of 12 without losing sound quality.

Germany's Fraunhofer Institute was the main developer of MPEG-1 Layer 3, and certain aspects of its MP3 work have patent protection approved in 1989 in Germany and in 1996 in the USA.

While MP3 is an open standard, meaning its source codes are freely available to would-be developers and controlled by no one, Fraunhofer and software developer Thomson Multimedia, which also holds MP3 patents, have claimed royalties must still be paid on certain encoding/decoding processes.

Fraunhofer sent letters in September, 1998 to several developers of encoders, asking for a licensing fee. The issue remained in contention as of late 1999.

But with MP3 players available for free on the Net (or requiring a modest fee under the "shareware" honor system), the format quickly gained popularity. With the advent of cheap encoding software from MusicMatch and the like, the ability to make an MP3 file became as simple as sticking a disc in a computer drive and clicking.

It should be noted that music lovers can legally copy a tape cassette or an MP3 file for personal use on a computer or portable player. But that copy cannot legally be given, traded, or sold to anyone else. It was the prolif-eration of fans posting popular songs to the Net and bla-tantly advertising their available collections for sharing that caused problems, rather than any outlaw function built into MP3.

Despite its superior audio quality and ease of transmission, MPEG did not immediately catch on with music fans after its introduction, that lag largely owing to the long download times caused by the slow-speed con-nections to the Internet owned by most of the population.

Instead, early web surfers were more enamored with streaming software, most prominently RealAudio made by Seattle's Progressive Networks, which allowed them to listen to audio transmissions on their computer without the need for cumbersome downloads.

However, research-oriented college campuses had superior speed connections already in place, and a curi-ous, music-hungry base of students who had grown up during the personal computer revolution.

That volatile combination would ignite the digital music revolution.

*   *   *

In 1993 in sleepy Santa Cruz, California, a hippie haven where the biggest stress comes from sunburn, two undergraduates were making the first moves into digital music.

Rob Lord and Jeff Patterson were music fans major-ing in computer and information science at the university. Acquaintances at Hart High School in their hometown of Valencia, California, they became fast friends in 1993 after Patterson transferred to Santa Cruz from Berkeley.

Patterson, a musician in the band Ugly Mugs, had made some awkward attempts at posting his music on the Net using MIDI and MOD files. When he arrived at Santa Cruz, Lord turned him on to MPEG, which was just start-ing to appear as a music distribution tool on tech-savvy college campuses.

"He told me about it in an e-mail he sent to me," Patterson recalled. "And so I convinced the guys in my band to spend $100 to go out and buy the software."

Not bound by fears of protecting corporation assets, Patterson and Lord quickly moved beyond the discussion groups and rudimentary music samples that had so far constituted the music industry's presence on the Internet.

After digitizing the Ugly Mugs using MP2, an earlier MPEG sound layer, several music clips were uploaded to the alt.binaries.multimedia and alt.binaries sound newsgroups. Lord and Patterson also provided a Xing Technologies MP2 player, since few in the newsgroups had the software.

The day after uploading the files, six people far from Santa Cruz responded with enthusiastic e-mails.

"The thing that interested us about it was the fact that these responses were from Turkey and Russia and all these places where they couldn't get ahold of Western music," Patterson said.

In the following days, more e-mails requesting music arrived. Soon, the news group discussions began requesting songs from other bands.

"We realized that all of a sudden I could upload all the songs from my tape, upload the (graphics) card from the CD, and have people download it all," said Patterson. "And some guy in Turkey has my demo tape and I didn't have to do anything to get it to him. They can make as many as they want and this was really important to us because we were all college students and completely broke and didn't have any way to press CDs or make tapes."

In November 1993, less than a month after the first uploads, the Internet Underground Music Archive was born. Lord and Patterson were shocked to discover that they were creating the first major music distribution site, which many established music industry types constantly predicted was years in the future.

The original idea was to position IUMA as an alternative distribution source for the music industry.

But in 1993 and 1994, the technological limitations were severe. 14.4 baud modems were still considered speedy, and many unfortunates had 2400 baud modems, the equivalent of the horse and buggy. To give an idea of speed's importance to the digital music community, consider that a 2400 baud modem took 14 hours to download a three-minute audio file, while a 28.8 modem would usually take 13 minutes. Using a high-speed cable modem, downloading a three-minute file takes 38 seconds.

IUMA used MPEG 2 compression, which meant it could take as long as a half-hour for a three-minute song to be downloaded over phone lines for most home users.

Finding a home for the site also proved a challenge. Initially, Lord and Patterson used an experimental site sponsored by Sun Microsystems in Chapel Hill, North Carolina, as their home server.

Santa Cruz was only interested in providing a small amount of space on its own campus server, although the administrators did give Lord and Patterson an office. "They were pretty strict about educational use only," said Patterson. But eventually the system migrated to the university.

Despite the small space on the Santa Cruz server, within IUMA's first year it was eating up "something like 70% to 80% of the bandwidth coming to Santa Cruz, something weird like that," Patterson recalled.

The college administrators weren't the only ones taking notice of IUMA. An article published in January, 1994 in the San Jose Mercury News brought a flood of publicity, and attracted the attention of Geffen Records and Warner Bros. Records.

Soon, Patterson and Lord were heading to L.A. for meetings. At Geffen, they would meet the man Patterson describes as "our mentor," a tall, maniacally passionate man who became one of the leaders of the digital music revolution.

*　　　　　　*　　　　　　*

Jim Griffin started out as a sports writer in Kentucky covering horse racing at the Lexington Herald-Leader, one of the first newspapers to create an online presence.

Griffin's curiosity about the online world and his interest in its issues led him to become involved with the Newspaper Guild, the national labor union governing print journalism. In late 1983, his enthusiasm for the emerging world of online journalism led him to a job in Washington, DC as an international representative for the Guild.

"I was easily the youngest guy on the staff at the time," Griffin recalled. "The other guys were like 50 and older. In other words, if you knew how a computer worked in a newsroom, you were unusual. So I got all the technology disputes. I learned a lot about how technology would impact entertainment by watching how it came to the journalism business first."

While visiting the San Diego News Tribune on business, Griffin took a side trip to see some friends in Los Angeles who worked in the music business. They took him to a party where he met executives from Geffen Records.

Griffin's knowledge about the online business intrigued the executives. They enlisted him to write some reports, which led to a two-month stint as a consultant to the company. In early 1992, Griffin was hired to spearhead Geffen's technology department, the first one in the record industry that was not devoted to obtaining tele-phones and basic computer use.

Instead, Griffin was given a mission: "They said we really want you to enable us to do things we could never do before. Specifically, we want you to enable us to figure out how to destroy our company and the industry in which it sits. There's some 14-year old kid out there who is trying to kill us and if you figure out who he is and how he's doing it before he kills us, maybe we can survive."

*   *   *

The meetings with the major labels were fruitful for IUMA. In addition to meeting Griffin, they were hired by Warner Bros. Records to create that company's web site.

"It was mainly curiosity, feeling us out, trying to figure out where all this was going and all that," Patterson recalls.

Despite the excitement of Hollywood – not to mention the free CDs that came with working for major labels – Patterson and Lord were worried.

"The indie community is a very sort of fickle community in that if you have any association with a major label, a lot of them will abandon you,"" Patterson said. But the lure of actually getting paid to play with their twin loves, music and computers, negated those nebulous fears.

The same could not be said for the record companies.

"Warner Bros. had a stance that this is great for unknown bands, but major bands are never going to be able to distribute their stuff electronically," said Patterson. "They basically said there's way too many security issues."

Patterson and Lord tried to explain that revenue models could shift away from a physical product that contains music to touring, merchandising, and subscription fees for access to music.

That advice met a stone wall.

"In our dealings around the industry and our limited discussions with ASCAP and BMI, we got the sense that when this started becoming noticeable in 1994, through probably '96 and '97, there was this attitude of the Internet is still just for geeks," Patterson said.

"It's just something going on, on campuses or something. It's not going to reach the mainstream. And I think people were just trying to ignore it, because it may have been possible to ignore at that point."

*   *   *

Despite the heads in the sand, there were some stirrings within the music industry that indicated someone was paying attention.

In what may have been the first lawsuit pitting the established music industry against technology, Frank Music Corp. filed a class-action suit on Nov. 29, 1993 in U.S. District Court in New York on behalf of itself and more than 140 music publisher members of the Harry Fox Agency against the online service CompuServe.

The suit said CompuServe's MIDI/Music Forum allowed subscribers to download and subsequently copy music files – including, according to court papers, "Unchained Melody" and 900 other songs – without the consent of the copyright owners.

(The suit was settled in 1995. CompuServe agreed to pay the Harry Fox Agency a lump sum of $568,000, or more than $600 for each song allegedly infringed. The money was divided among the publishers pursuing the suit. CompuServe made no admission of liability in the settlement).

By 1993, most major record labels had discussed digital music, but it was regarded as a far-off, nebulous concept.

"The companies had, for a long time – individually, in their own way – been looking at what digital delivery was going to mean for them," said David Leibowitz, former executive VP and general counsel at RIAA and later CEO of Aris Technologies, which specializes in digital watermarking. "Some were more far-sighted than others.But each had different individual efforts underway to deal with digital delivery from their own perspective. The objective was to be pro-company so that they would be able to maintain and serve their customers, ideally in a way that's not threatening to retail."

The problem, said Leibowitz, was that while those slow, cautious parliaments were in session, MP3 was revolutionary. "It's really been a catalyst causing a dramatic acceleration of their processes, heightening the urgency to get their acts in gear."

Others were less charitable.

"To say that the industry understood what was happening to it would be giving them a lot more credit than they were evidencing or even are evidencing or starting to evidence now," said Jim Griffin. "I don't think they understood fundamentally what was happening."

"I think there were a few people at the RIAA who might have understood it," Griffin added. "But they weren't the people that were listening to music on their desktop. You have to remember that entertainment companies didn't even have computers on the average person's desk in 1993, 1994, 1995 or 1996. It's very, very hard to understand the future unless you participate in it. If you can at least send music down the hall, you would understand how it would be sent around the world."

The Recording Industry Assn. of America had contemplated digital deliveries and made provisions for same as early as the work that resulted in passage of the Digital Performance Rights in Sound Recordings Act of 1995.

But much as residents sometimes take a laissez-faire approach to disaster preparation in earthquake-prone Southern California, the record industry was caught ill-prepared by the suddenness with which MP3 exploded onto the scene.

The piracy arm of the industry, housed in the RIAA, relied on a network of semi-retired policemen trained to go to flea markets and sniff out counterfeit cassettes and CDs. They were not, to be frank, computer savvy.

Some voices within the RIAA were aware of the rising online problem. Younger workers, far down the food chain, were asking their superiors if they knew about certain songs on line.

Part of the problem with the RIAA's seemingly slow reaction also had to do with the nature of the organization. In order to formulate a plan of attack, the organization has to bring a problem to the attention of its membership and then ask how they want it handled. With little evidence that such online piracy posed an immediate threat, and with the industry still booming in the early '90s, few companies were alarmed.

"Everybody knew there was going to be a legitimate (online music) business and everybody was trying to figure out what that would be," said RIAA CEO Hilary Rosen, reflecting back on the moment. "The earlier issues, discussions, and debates were about how much should we work together as an industry to develop the legitimate business, because there was still uncertainty about what would be proprietary and what would need to be standardized. And people really didn't have the answers to that."

What the industry did do, Rosen said, was lay some early groundwork for what would later become the Secure Digital Music Initiative, a coalition of record, consumer electronics, and affiliated businesses attempting to devise a secure online architecture for digital music.

"This was all before MP3," Rosen said. "Everybody talks about SDMI as a reaction to MP3, but really it was sort of in anticipation of the legitimate market."

The industry meetings focused on two features that were most important for standardization of online delivery.

One was ease of use, "so that if somebody wanted

to buy a Madonna record online they wouldn't have to have a different kind of player than if they wanted to buy a Mariah Carey record," Rosen said.

The other was less well-defined, a method of encryption that would outline how a piece of digital music would be purchased. Options ranged from pay-per-play jukebox scenarios to permanent downloads.

"Our thinking was much more transactionally-oriented," Rosen said. "But the idea was that if you could deal with the transaction, you were dealing with the security."

But with the online delivery of music envisioned as arriving about the same time a hotel opened on Mars, there was little incentive beyond drawing-board plans.

Then MP3 hit like a hurricane.

It was late 1996 when Rosen sat down with Frank Creighton, at the time the RIAA director of investigations and initiator of the organization's Internet enforcement program.

Rosen, speaking at the 1999 Plug.In digital music conference in New York, said Creighton was "basically explaining to me how many MPEG compression files they were finding and how many sessions (computer users) were actually sending. We were clearly not ready as an industry to entice customers away from these files and into the more legitimate marketplace."

The timing was not good for Rosen, who was about to ascend to the RIAA's highest office. "I thought, "Oh shit. I'm about to be named CEO and the whole industry is turning upside down. All of this will hit the fan just as I'm named CEO in July."

In fact, she said, "that's sort of what happened."

Rosen used an analogy borrowed from American history – and, she said, from veteran record executive Marc Geiger, the cofounder of the ARTISTdirect digital music company – to explain the state of the recording business at that moment.

"The railroads should have been GM and Ford and Chrysler, but they didn't think anybody would want to travel off the tracks," said Rosen. "The telephone companies should have been the cellular phone companies, but they couldn't imagine anybody wanting to talk on the phone in their cars. And then, of course, the networks are the best example most recently. They also should have owned the cable industry but they couldn't imagine what anyone would want to do watching all those channels."

It was clear, Rosen said, that the record companies didn't want to be in that position. "But it was possible we were heading there if we were not moving quickly enough in a coordinated fashion."

The first step by the RIAA was to hire a consultant group to help with their plans. They recommended several ideas "for how we can try and create a win-win with the technology and creative community," Rosen said. "It was very clear at the time that many people in the technology industry were sort of laughing at the notion of selling music online."

In essence, the technology industry was speaking from experience, having long ago fought its own battle with encryption, only to abandon it.

Rosen recalled their message: "Your artists are probably just going to have to figure out how to go on tour or sell their underwear once they've recorded this song because there's no way to sell music on the Internet. The Internet is all about everything being free."

Physical Goods in Virtual Stores

A t the same time the online digital music world was developing, the record industry was enamored with something that seemed to offer the promise of digital music and multimedia in a form they were more familiar with.

The Enhanced CD, also known as CD Plus and several other names, was the recording industry's moniker for a new form of compact disc that combined multimedia features with full CD sound. In the early stages of its roll-out, some believed the Enhanced CD would someday make audio-only discs obsolete.

That hope, born of the same economic conditions and stagnant artistry that birthed the compact disc, was based mostly on anticipation of a new sales windfall. Expected to cost between $20 to $27 per disc, the Enhanced CD would be priced roughly $10 above the standard CD, but in the range of low-end CD-ROMS.

Plans for an RIAA-sponsored compilation disc

accompanied by a massive consumer education campaign designed to lure those who just purchased CD-ROM drives were afoot. Industry pundits salivated at the prospect of a new world of computer users augmenting their collections.

There was just one problem: nobody wanted the discs.

Consumers just recovering from replacing their vinyl record collection were wary, even though the discs could be played on regular CD players, unveiling their multimedia features only when inserted into a CD-ROM drive.

Part of the problem with the Enhanced CD rollout may have been consumer confusion. Various audio titles with multimedia capability were released as "AudioVision CDs" and "Enhanced CDs" by independent record companies.

Meanwhile, the Recording Industry Assn. of America, the industry trade group that represents the majority of large record companies, mulled whether to call its product CD Plus. Eventually, the discs became generally known as ECD, although some labels still refused to embrace the term.

Even if the terminology was uniform, there was little compelling content on most Enhanced CDs.

Lisa Lewis, then a senior director at Music Marketing Network, an independent consultant to the record industry in the mid-1990s and later a marketer with Universal Music, voiced aloud what was being murmured behind closed doors throughout the industry. She noted that consumers were being quickly turned off by inferior products.

"If they're going to spend $19-$29, and if they can only use it once and it only gives a discography, are you really going to buy any more than one artist?" Lewis asked.

In some cases, artists themselves needed an introduction to the product.

Typical was Kitaro, a Japanese new age artist whose "Kitaro: An Enchanted Evening" was released as one of the first Enhanced CDs.

Kitaro admitted he did not closely follow the construction of the features on his disc, a lack of concern typical of other artists exploring the new format. "My company kind of put in an interview section," he said. "I didn't know (about) that. We put it on, and, "Wow!"

"That's why CD-ROMs have never been as successful as they should be," said Charles Como, one of the early multimedia designers for the record industry. "People are afraid of technology. So what they do is hand it to some kids up in San Francisco and go, "Here. This is Sting. Go make something."

Such surprises generally didn't lead to greatness, although several Enhanced CDs by Bush and Primus scored relatively high critical marks.

Some two years after the first product hit the market, Enhanced CDs were plagued by lack of support at retail and by manufacturers; release date slippage; price cutting; and, most glaring, technical problems that made many older discs incompatible with CD-ROM drives.

ECDs created using the pre-gap (also known as track zero) method, which encodes the multimedia elements in a hidden file contained between index points zero and one on a conventional audio CD, were rendered inoperative because of changes made to Windows 95.

Microsoft, in the course of updating Windows 95 after its much-balleyhooed launch, disabled the software's ability to play the multimedia portion of all pre-gap encoded ECDs. Thus, newer titles by Soundgarden and Monster Magnet, to name two plagued with the problem, didn't work in many machines.

Who ultimately killed ECD's chances in the market? Finger-pointing abounded.

"Nobody cares!" said retailer Dave Sparks, the owner of Interact!, a Pasadena, Calif.-based CD-ROM store, describing the customer reaction to ECD. His remarks were repeated, in less blunt terms, by retailers, distributors, record company executives and industry consultants.

Duncan Kennedy of Apple Computers, which had a web site devoted to Enhanced CDs and actively pushed the format, says the record industry "did a terrible job of marketing and introducing them. The confusion didn't help the consumer."

Ultimately, the record industry may have created its own version of the Betamax, a product that was technically superior, but one that consumers feared to purchase.

Marc Schiller, former head of House of Blues New Media and later head of Internet marketing firm Electric Artists, summed it up.

"Unless there is a major marketing push behind something new, the public is wary about going into what they consider a fringe product because they don't know whether it's going to be supported," he said. "It's a logical fear."

*   *   *

At the dawn of the commercial age of the Internet, several efforts were made to transplant the world of music retailing to cyberspace.

CDNow was started by twin brothers Jason and Matt Olim in February of 1994, and launched with a TelNet, text-only site in August, 1994, switching to a web site at the end of that year.

Jason Olim was a Brown computer science graduate who worked as a software engineer before founding his company. His brother was an astrophysics major at Columbia University.

"I spent a lot of time in stores," said Jason Olim. "For me, the key was solving the information problem."

Olim was a frequent customer of Tower Records on

Newbury Street in Boston during his undergraduate days. He remembered one of the dilemmas of his shopping experience that made an impact on his future.

"I had bought "Kind Of Blue" by Miles Davis," Olim recalled. "I go to the guy behind the counter, "You've got 15 other Miles Davis albums in the rack here. What other album do I want?"

The clerk's answer, predictable to anyone who frequents a record store: "I dunno." That inadvertent remark planted the seed of a multimillion dollar online business.

"I ended up buying "Bitches Brew," Olim said. "And that really ruined my day. It took me years to get into "Bitches Brew." I like it now, but back then, you've got a guy listening to "Kind of Blue" and then you get this really tricked-up stuff."

To counter future problems, Olim developed the habit of walking around the store with a record guide. It struck him that the perfect online business was matching a music catalog with a guide. Securing an investment from Alan Meltzer of Alliance Entertainment Corp., the brothers began their company.

The Olims in general were young Internet entrepreneurs to the max. Jason, in particular, was perceived by some veterans as wide-eyed and bushy-tailed.

"But he thinks that being in the music business is really cool," said one observer. "And he keeps sort of going back to his own musical references to point out how cool it is. I think the guy's just a hi-tech geek and loved music and was good at computers and saw an opportunity to break ground and he did so."

The atmosphere at CDNow was heavy on beating the competition, so much so that the direct competitor in the space, N2K, was made into something of a Great Satan, its every move watched closely, its executives scorned behind closed doors, and its every failure cheered. "That was very much a part of the corporate culture," said one insider.

The Olims' outsider status was reinforced, to a degree, by the company's location. Started in the basement of their parents' home in the tiny Philadelphia suburb of Ambler, Pennsylvania with a $20,000 initial investment, CDNow was located in the mainstream music business equivalent of Istanbul.

The 1997 National Assn. of Recording Merchandisers (NARM) convention in San Francisco would prove just how far outside.

CDNow had angered traditional brick and mortar retailers several times that year. Eager to differentiate themselves, the Olims had made store personnel a particular target in their media interviews.

But the biggest faux pas by traditional music industry standards came when CDNow began advertising a big sale on Grammy winning titles for 50% off list price. The plan was to offer a four-day discount on 80 titles, with the hope that new customers would discover CDNow. The online store had not previously been attracting those interested in the hits, Olim said. "80% of what we sell is not in the Top 1000," he said in 1997.

The discount lowered most $16.98 suggested retail price albums below the minimum-advertised price policies of the major record distributors. The policies required that retailers sell CDs no lower than the MAP price if they expected to get co-op advertising dollars from the distributors.

CDNow, which obtained its stock from a wholesaler in Woodland Hills, Calif., did not get any co-op advertising dollars, so it was not bound by MAP guidelines.

The big boys were horrified, and blasted CDNow in the press, claiming the company was devaluing music, and warned that there would be consequences.

"We spent millions dollars on ads around the Grammys, TV ads, print, radio," Olim said in a later interview on the Grammy plan. "You don't do that without something really over the top to convert that noise to action."

Although the online discounts were not huge, particularly when shipping costs borne by consumers were factored, they threatened the older players in the game, who were having a rough time that year.

January of 1997 was particularly troublesome for music retailers. With sales flat in music for most of 1996, the post-Christmas season threatened to bring a flood of returns and missed payments by retailers to record companies in the millions of dollars.

In a stark reminder of the delicate partnership between record companies and their customers, the big six record distributors in the U.S. had to agree to extend terms-of-credit and back-off on calling in past due accounts for Musicland, the nation's biggest record chain.

Essentially, the distributors were betting that Musicland would avoid bankruptcy, a domino that likely would cause other troubled record chains to topple. That would result in record companies receiving pennies on the dollar for their already-shipped goods, a disaster in an already financially-precarious period, one that saw many brick and mortar retailers consolidating operations by closing under-performing stores and laying off employees.

Thus, they were particularly eager to cash in on the annual bonanza that comes from Grammy season, a traditionally slow time of year. Anything that would slice away that pie – and certainly customers that could watch the Grammy TV broadcast and order immediately on their computer was a potential dagger – was striking at the heart of the establishment.

The Olims, making their first appearance that year at the NARM convention, traditionally the senior prom of the music industry, were given the cold shoulder by many key retail executives. Musicland CEO Jack Eugster literally walked away when introduced. Tower Records chairman Russ Solomon was slightly more cordial, but told Jason Olim that he didn't like what he was doing.

Olim was prepared not to be greeted warmly, but was still taken aback by the obvious hostility in the air toward him and his venture. To lighten the tension, he attempted to make a joke out of his reception during the convention's opening day.

During a panel concerning online retailing, he appeared wearing a Philadelphia Eagles football helmet, noting to the assembled that he was prepared for the anticipated battering.

The tactic worked. By the third day of the convention, Olim was able to engage his fellow conventioneers in a discussion in which he tried to emphasize his argument that his tactics would only expand the market for all, a hard point to believe given that CDNow's mission was to change the way the consumer purchased music.

Away from NARM, even Olim admitted that. "The contraction in the market benefitted us to the extent that a lot of retail shops closing down forced people to have to learn to switch," said Olim.

"So we got the advantage of that customer saying, "Okay. I've got to look for a place to buy music."

*   *   *

Competing against the Olim brothers in the online arena were two figures from the traditional record industry, albeit the more maverick side of the business.

By the time they entered the online world by investing in the tiny Brooklyn-based multimedia firm N2K (an acronym for Need To Know) and starting an online retailer, Music Boulevard, Larry Rosen and Dave Grusin were already the successful cofounders of GRP Records, one of the first record companies to issue works on compact disc.

Rosen started his music career as a session drummer and recording engineer in a studio he built himself. In

1972, he began working with multi-instrumentalist/ vocalist Jon Lucien, who asked keyboardist Dave Grusin to write some charts to go along with the tracks Rosen had recorded.

"That's when we really started working in the studio together as joint producers," said Rosen. "That turned into Grusin/Rosen Productions, which turned into GRP Records."

Striking a deal with Arista for their newly-formed imprint, the team quickly built a reputation for cutting-edge jazz.

In late 1978, Rosen read about Dr. Tom Stockom from MIT translating analog signal into digital sound. "I got in touch with him and I flew his people and this machine in from Salt Lake City, where it was all housed, to try it on for a recording session," Rosen said. The session in question was for Grusin's "Mountain Dance."

The problem with digital recording at that point was its relatively primitive state. The digital machines offered only two tracks for recording, as opposed to the then-standard 24 or more track studios.

Rosen and Grusin weren't sure how it would work, so they hedged their bets. Rosen would do a live mix of the recording session for "Mountain Dance" using the digital two-track recording equipment, backed up with a simultaneous recording on the 24-track board.

"I remember going to the studio to hear a playback and realizing that we were used to hearing tape noise before we hear the notes," said Grusin. "And this was like absolute blackness and all of a sudden this piece of light hit without any warning. It was incredible."

The two were so blown away that they finished "Mountain Dance" by recording directly with the two-track digital recorder, one of the first entirely digital recordings.

"It was one of those kind of things like the light bulb

goes off," Rosen said of the experience. "We heard that sound and we said, "This is absolutely incredible. The clarity of the sound, the fullness of it, the punch of it....we were just so taken by the digital technology, we said, "This is it." Everything we were going to do is going to be in the digital domain."

Of course, there was one additional problem. At the time of this discovery, there were no compact discs. The GRP digital recordings were therefore issued on vinyl, which Rosen claimed still sounded better because sound was not degraded in the mixing process, a problem typical for analog recordings.

Of course, digital recordings were also more expensive. Under terms of its Arista deal, GRP had its logo on the label, but all recording costs were funded by Arista. Except for a few odd reversion clauses where the master recordings remained with the artist, most of the records recorded by GRP were also owned by Arista.

That would prove to be a problem.

By 1979, the great record industry post-disco slump had hit the business. Arista accountants approached Grusin and Rosen.

"We don't see any reason for you guys to be bringing in this digital equipment, since people are only buying LPs anyway," Rosen recalled being told at the meeting. "What difference does it really make? And we could save $7500 for every record if you guys weren't insisting on this digital stuff."

Rosen and Grusin were adamant. It had to be digital.

The debate ended in an amicable split with Arista. Grusin and Rosen formed their own independent GRP label with the idea that every record would be digital.

"I went back to Arista as soon as we started the company and said, "You know all those masters that we made? I want to buy them back from you and have the CD rights for that." And they said, "Sure. Who's going to ever buy CDs?"

The six-title catalog purchase laid a solid foundation for GRP, which eventually was so successful, it was purchased on Feb. 28, 1990 for shares of MCA Inc. common stock valued at $40 million.

Rosen and Grusin took a vacation, then looked for a new project. Rosen quickly found one – he hired N2K to make a CD-ROM, but soon became enamored of the fledgling company. He made an investment and took on a new role as a multimedia mogul.

Grusin wasn't so sure. "But my partner, who can't sit still at all, jumped into this new thing. I got very nervous about involving myself in a technology that I really didn't totally understand. But what always convinces me is my partner's enthusiasm and kind of positive attitude about all this kind of stuff. And I decided, well, why not? I'm not going to buy a Winnebago and retire."

Rosen felt the online world provided the perfect way to connect the music industry to customers.

"In all these years of running record companies, the one thing that you really understand is that you really don't know the music buyer directly on a one-to-one basis," said Rosen. "The thing I thought about the Internet is if you have the ability to really understand and have a relationship one to one with the buyer, what a strategic advantage that would give you."

Ultimately, Rosen envisioned the Net as a distribution medium.

"You'll distribute these bits right to them, right to their home, and they're going to make their own CD in their own house, whether it's stored on a CD or a DVD or a flash memory. That's what I felt about it from the beginning. And that's certainly what the whole idea of this company is about."

    *   *   *

Oddly, a recording industry that vociferously objected to digital transmissions of songs had no problem with online music sellers who violated laws by shipping compact discs all over the world.

So-called "parallel imports" are defined as goods made in one country and shipped into another country, usually without the authorization of the intellectual property rights owner in the receiving country. In the case of recorded music, someone who manufactured a recording in the United States, for example, could not ship that recording to France without the assent of the French copyright holder, usually another record company.

Although some foreign recordings have different packaging design and music than their U.S. cousins, generally the two products would compete with each other. Parallel import laws were designed to prevent that. Application of the law killed the market in imported records in the U.S.

Yet online retailers selling compact discs to a worldwide audience – often at prices greatly reduced from that available on foreign store shelves – faced no opposition.

The key was the type of product the online stores were selling. Most of their business was in jazz, classical, and hard-to-find catalog items, most not found on store shelves in the U.S. or overseas.

"I'm concerned about it, because as a practical matter, they are violating our companies' rights," said RIAA CEO Hilary Rosen, asked about the practice during a 1997 interview. "I think, though, that this is a problem that has the potential to take care of itself over the long-term. But the record companies clearly have the power to be more strict about their enforcement now. And they're not."

In short, because the new online world was perceived as supplementing the existing market structure rather than challenging it, violating the law was given a wink and a nod by the record companies.

*   *   *

At the same time the music retail world made its first tentative steps onto the Internet, the real action was in programming the web sites.

Instead of a screenplay tucked into a drawer, suddenly Hollywood's gold rush focused on the World Wide Web. Record labels tripped over themselves searching out someone who could set-up and design their own on-ramp to the information superhighway, and they were willing to pay well for it.

"We actually had two businesses going at once," said Jeff Patterson of IUMA, who designed the Warner Bros. site, among other projects. "We were digitizing and distributing independent music. And then we were also running a consulting house. We would build sites like the Van Halen universe site. We built the original Egghead demo site. Some weird things that you wouldn't think we'd do. But we did that stuff just to pay the bills."

Charles Como, a former stockbroker turned Internet entrepreneur, worked with IUMA and others in the early years of web design. He quickly became one of the must-have names in record company rolodexes.

Among his favorite tasks during that period was helping create "Megadeth, Arizona," the artificial desert town devoted to the speed metal band.

"We put in Megadeth, Arizona and we started promoting it a little bit on the Net," recalled Como. "Next thing you know, we're getting 15,000 log-ins a day. Then we were on MTV for a little splurt, then it got 25,000 log-ins a day. And then all of a sudden, it's getting 35,000 log-ins a day."

One Halloween promotion was particularly memorable, and is an example of the Net's reach even at that early stage of development.

"I tell people on the Internet to come into this thing called the Megadiner, a little chat room I created," Como said. "I set up the computers at 10 a.m., and kids were logging in from Norway and Australia, asking "Where's the band?" I'm telling them they have to wait like 14 hours."

Dave Mustaine of Megadeth became a particularly ardent fan of the Net. "That Saturday, he spends six hours in the Megadiner talking to his fans," Como said. "On Sunday, literally the guy gets up at 7:30 in the morning and spends 14 hours in the Megadiner talking to his fans."

Another early Net-head was Seal, according to Como.

"So he comes over and he looks at this Internet thing and I show him CUseeMe (a software that allows video conferencing) and he's like, "This is amazing." And all of a sudden he starts coming over on a regular basis. It's like a Sunday afternoon, he comes and sits down with me. We run the CUseeMe and there's somebody in New York, in Japan, Australia, and this girl in Utah, her name's Alex. She goes, "Is that you, Seal?" She runs out of the room and you could tell she put lipstick on. "Can you sing me a song?" And he starts singing. There's some people in Moscow, in New York, just listening. It was the coolest thing, and there's just 15 people listening to this."

Big money was starting to fly around for site creators.

"We are potentially changing the way things are, and if you have some big corporation coming to you and saying we want you to help us out, I'd say, 'Well, your services are very valuable to them'," Como said. "You need to make sure that you're getting paid what you should be getting paid."

That was often far more than the site creators ever dreamed. "I had negative $143 in my account when Capitol Records cut me a check," Como recalled. "I would have taken anything, $500.....but it ended up being a hell of a lot more than that."

*   *   *

The age of experimentation was upon the Net, but the experiments were still cautious. No one was willing to put content up because of fears of piracy.

"When I first arrived at Geffen in 1993," said Jim Griffin, "one of the first questions I was asked by everyone was, "When can we put full-length songs online?"

Griffin told his bosses that it was entirely possible to do that very thing at that moment.

So they did.

Obtaining the right song took some work. "At first, they got me a Sammy Hagar song that was like six minutes long," recalled Griffin, a length that would have turned off the average 2400 baud modem user. The next offering was an Aerosmith b-side track that had never been released. "Head First" was "only three minutes and something long," said Griffin. "So I spent the Memorial Day weekend digitizing the song."

Griffin tried many encoding combinations to achieve the proper fidelity. "We would do it in mono, would we do it in stereo, would we do it 22 kilohertz, 11 khz, 44 khz. We settled on 22 khz, because we figured that was as small we were going to be able to make it and still retain quality."

The file format was also a crucial selection. "We settled on the .wav format because, at the time, .wav was the most universal format," said Griffin. "You didn't need a player. If you just double clicked on it in Windows, it started playing."

On June 14, 1994, Aerosmith's "Head First" was posted on CompuServe for one week. "Within the first day it went through 10,000 downloads and was on the cover of most major newspapers," Griffin said. "We realized we were on to something."

There was, however, a problem.

"Our parent company was not that pleased," said Griffin, referring to MCA Music Entertainment, now Universal Music Group. "At Geffen we felt quite good about it, everybody did. But Universal said, "Wait a minute. What are you doing?" I am not going into who they were but I'll just say that the parent company was very concerned that we were letting the cat out of a big bag."

The attitude, Griffin said, was not uncommon in the record industry as a whole. Griffin described it as "let's keep the franchise together as long as we can and not turn the means of production, or at least distribution, over to people."

But the future was arriving even faster than they feared.

Means of Transmission

L ogic dictated that in a world moving inexorably toward digital distribution but without any security, someone would invent a security system.

Someone turned out to be Liquid Audio, a Redwood, City, Calif. upstart, and a2b Music, a spawn of AT&T.

Liquid Audio was founded by Gerry Kearby, who took a long, strange trip to the world of digital music.

Kearby's resume lists stints as a drummer, Marine, audio engineering and broadcasting major at radical San Francisco State, Disneyland band member, sound engineer for the Grateful Dead, custom designer of audio/visual equipment for George Lucas, and Wyoming school teacher.

In 1980, Kearby arrived in Redwood City, Calif., the Mecca of audio recording thanks to the residency of Ampex, at the time the premiere audio recording equipment company. He came to assist a friend in constructing a $10 million teleproduction facility.

What he planted were the seeds of his future business.

"In the process of doing that, we learned a lot about sort of what we thought was going to be the coming revolution," recalled Kearby. "The people who were running this studio had a lot of visions for how they would like to have computer control of it. But this was 1980, and maybe you could get a deck or something, but there were no personal computers. So we began to build computer control of the switching and routing and video editing gear."

From there, Kearby did work at Apple and Stanford's Center for Computer Research in Music and Acoustics, nicknamed CARMA. George Lucas was paying attention to the development of digital tools, and recruited Kearby and others to build digital audio tools for film.

When that ended, Kearby created a company based around the tools he had created. But in the late 1980s, he sold that company and worked for a few years for its successor, Studer Revox. He then took a year off from work, "walking my dog and listening to the O.J. trial," he said.

Kearby had a vague idea to take his professional tools and techniques and apply them to digital music distribution, but needed to focus on exactly how he would initiate his efforts.

A meeting with superstar venture capitalist Ann Winblad put it in perspective.

Kearby had to jump through hoops to get his meeting.

The Center for Software Development, a San Jose, Calif. non-profit where entrepreneurial companies can go and get their software tested and learn business development, sponsored an annual fundraiser called "Meet A Venture Capitalist." For $25, contestants on what the VC people jokingly referred to as "The Gong Show" had fifteen minutes to pitch their ideas.

"I called down there and said I'd like to meet Ann Winblad and they said, "That's been sold out for months,"

Kearby said. "So I said, 'Well, did anyone cancel?' "No." Well, I thought for a second. Everyone that's going there is looking for money. I said, "Did anybody's check bounce?"

Somebody's did. Kearby got his meeting.

Winblad liked the idea of digital music distribution, but needed further proof. She asked Kearby to get an exclusive pact with renowned audio firm Dolby Labs for its technology.

There was one hangup – Dolby was a licensing company that did not grant exclusives.

Kearby decided to place a bet. A familiar face to Dolby through his audio engineering ventures, he managed to get a meeting. He bet the Dolby executives that his new chief technology officer, Phil Wiser, could devise a way to improve Dolby's AC3 sound processor. If Wiser did, Dolby would grant Liquid Audio exclusive rights to the Internet in return for the improvement.

They said, "Well, that's a safe bet," said Kearby. 'He can't know anything we don't know.' "So we shook hands on the bet."

But Wiser had been working on Dolby products and had some ideas. Finally, in what Kearby describes as akin to an oral Ph.D exam, Wiser faced off with eight Dolby engineers with their arms crossed, staring gruffly.

"It took about four hours, and phrases like noise to mask ratio and things were flying around, things I didn't even know what the hell they were talking about," Kearby said.

At the end of the presentation, the heads of Dolby looked at each other.

They said, "Well, he's right. He thought of something we hadn't thought of," Kearby said. The deal was on.

Winblad lived up to her part of the deal, closing on $2 million in venture funding shortly after.

*　　　　　　　*　　　　　　　*

Initially, Liquid Audio had two business plans. One was a patented application for compressing audio and putting it on a CD-ROM, where users could remix the audio. That was the main pitch to venture capitalists, who envisioned a product that would, for example, allow computer users to slow down a Jimi Hendrix guitar solo, learn it note for note, then eliminate the lead guitar on the track and play along with the band.

The technology also would work on the Net. But the CD-ROM was the current darling of the multimedia world. "We just didn't think that anybody would fund a company that early on for music distribution," said Kearby.

Liquid Audio opened its doors in May, 1996, and debuted that November at its first trade show, the Audio Engineering Society's annual gathering.

Sammy Hagar, friendly with many of the Liquid Audio personnel, donated a song to put up on the Net for a streaming audio demonstration.

The title was somewhat ironic. "Salvation on Sand Hill" might have been construed as a reference to the street where many Silicon Valley venture capitalists reside. Instead, Hagar's song referred to religious snake-handlers.

Liquid Audio initially touted its technology as a production tool for studios, A&R personnel, and salesmen. The strategy was to build a relationship with key entertainment companies. Then, when digital distribution arrived, they would already have partners in that business.

The debut was a hit. But Liquid Audio was merely streaming. The big breakthrough in music distribution was envisioned as digital downloading. And to do that, Liquid Audio aligned with a partner, New York's N2K, parent of the Music Boulevard.com site, and began to work on putting the concept into action.

"They had a vision that they wanted to sell downloadable songs," said Kearby of N2K, chosen because of an experiment earlier in 1997, a free digital download from David Bowie, "Telling Lies," that saw over 300,000 downloads in a week. The staggering total showed both the penetration of the Internet with consumers and the audience's eagerness for any music by popular artists.

"Trade shows are the natural nodes that we use for milestones," said Kearby. "We had Plug.In (a seminar sponsored by New York research firm Jupiter Communications) in July, 1997, as our goal to have the first downloadable songs up for sale, encrypted, all the e-commerce pieces done and the CD burning piece done. So we just put our heads down and ran for that date as fast as we could."

   *   *   *

While downloading caused the music industry anxiety, there was a much warmer embrace for streaming media.

Streaming media didn't require users to download a file. Shortly after clicking on a sound file icon, users could begin listening while the rest of the data was being transmitted.

While that function eliminated the sometimes interminable wait for a download, streaming was not without its own faults. The sound quality in earlier versions of streaming media left a lot to be desired, and the stream was often interrupted in mid-song by congestion on the Net, which blocked the data from its downstream path.

The first major streaming audio player was Seattle's Progressive Networks, later to change its name to RealNetworks, creators of RealAudio and later RealVideo and the RealJukebox. The company opened its doors in 1995, with version 1.0 of RealAudio bowing that same year. By 1999, the company's RealPlayer (which was used by consumers to play the audio and video files) had 61 million users and controlled well over 80% of the streaming media market.

The company was founded by Rob Glaser, a former ten-year Microsoft employee and the company's youngest vice president ever at the time of his employment.

Glaser managed Microsoft Word and networking, then moved to its Multimedia and Consumer Systems group, where a corporate power struggle resulted in his leaving the company.

Despite licensing his technology to his former employer – a move that briefly backfired when Microsoft released a competing audio/video player – Glaser would later pay back the software giant by testifying against its allegedly predatory engineering and marketing practices during the Senate Judiciary Committee's Competition in the Digital Age hearings.

Despite its affinity for streaming, RealNetworks would later enter the downloading space in a big way. It acquired Xing Technology, one of the early developers of MP3 technology, announced a deal with IBM to develop a secure digital distribution format, and then launched RealJukebox, which allows users to download, store and manage MP3 files and other music formats. The software also encodes CDs to digital file formats, including converting them to MP3s, creating a sore spot with the record industry.

Not that such problems mattered. At a RealNetworks convention in the summer of 1999, Glaser reported RealJukebox had more than 100,000 downloads in its first day and 250,000 after two days.

Clearly, consumers were demanding their MP3.

*   *   *

About the same time Liquid Audio launched, corporate giant AT&T also threw its hat into the digital downloading arena.

Larry Miller was COO of a2b Music, the division charged with developing the AT&T strategy to launch audio compression and security technology developed in its labs into the music business mainstream.

"We took those core assets and turned them into a business in a way that the record industry would view as being creative or value-added for them, rather than competitive or threatening or anything that would have a negative connotation," said Miller.

AT&T largely kept its hand off a2b, hoping the company could operate on Internet speed rather than the pace of a telecommunications behemoth.

Miller came from a media background. "I had grown up in the radio business," he said, serving as a DJ before moving into station management. One his greatest triumphs was being part of the management team that helped WHTZ conquer the New York metropolitan area in 1983, going from worst to first, as the station's motto proudly proclaimed of an Arbitron ratings triumph that became a legend in the radio business.

But Miller was restless with radio. By chance, he saw the first issue of Wired magazine, on sale in the Tribune Building in Manhattan, home of the New York Daily News at the time.

"I thought, "Oh, my God. This could be the most important magazine in the world right now. This is an unbelievable opportunity."

Miller first seized that opportunity by working in management consulting, helping large media and entertainment companies conceive their Internet strategy. One of the companies seeking to devise a strategy was AT&T Solutions, which was looking for a head of media and entertainment.

In 1995, Miller was the man they tapped for what, after the AT&T divestiture, would become a2b, an end-to-end music industry solution for digital downloading based on the Advanced Audio Coding (AAC) algorithms.

The artists working with a2b included such hitmakers as Lenny Kravitz, Tori Amos, and the Verve Pipe.

"We've always believed of the few key drivers for there to be a really robust electronic distribution channel in this industry is that lots and lots of music from artists we know and love needs to be made available," said Miller. "You've got to embrace the incumbents in today's music industry in order to make a place for yourself in this new world."

That world arrived in the summer of 1997.

*   *   *

The first session of the Jupiter Communications Plug.In convention, held in Manhattan in July, 1997 as part of the Intel New York Music Festival, opened with a bang.

Claude Leglise, a senior executive with Intel working on the convention, found out that the future was a lot closer than his own timetable for digital downloading.

Prompted on a digital distribution panel during the opening session to estimate when downloading of recordings would happen, Leglise estimated it was at least five years in the future.

Sitting next to him on the dais was Larry Rosen, chairman/CEO of N2K Music.

Rosen paused a beat.

"We're starting today," he said.

Indeed, the long-awaited dawn of digital downloading had arrived. On July 16 at 6 p.m. EST, N2K (Need to Know, somewhat ironic in light of the Intel man's comments), became the first company to sell secure, digitally-downloaded, CD-quality singles from prominent recording artists.

For 99 cents apiece, consumers visiting N2K's Music Boulevard site (www.musicblvd.com) after Rosen's epic announcement found 15 different singles from the likes of Chick Corea, Jonathan Butler, Richard Barone, Stewart Copeland, and others.

The sale required users to first download a free player devised by Liquid Audio. They then were able to preview the music, and, if they decided to purchase, immediately download the song to their computer's hard drive.

Once on the hard drive, the consumer could either listen to it through their PC's sound system or, with the addition of a $500 unit from Philips Electronics, copy the music onto a CD-Recordable (CD-R) disc that could be played in a standard CD player.

(Another company, Sightsound Inc., claims it sold an unencrypted song in 1995 via digital download from a Pittsburgh band later signed to Atlantic Records, the Gathering Field.

The company is better known for winning a patent in 1993 titled "Method for Transmitting a Desired Digital Video or Audio Signal," which ostensibly gives them the right to collect a fee for each download on the Net. The company has since pursued its patent claims, despite much skepticism from record labels and studios. "It was like saying you have a patent on oxygen," attorney Eric Kronfeld told the Wall Street Journal. Although several companies have agreed to license the patented process, the issue remained largely unresolved as of late 1999).

The N2K e_mod system was finalized the night before Rosen's momentous announcement.

"We were burning the midnight oil and regretting (the demise of) the days of easy access to amphetamine sulfate because we didn't have that thing working until the night before," said Gerry Kearby of Liquid Audio. "It was around 11:00 at night before it worked."

Present at the N2K offices in lower Manhattan were Larry Rosen, Kearby, producer Phil Ramone, and assorted executives from both companies.

"We had all the bosses of N2K in Chris Bell's office," said Kearby. After numerous errors, they finally managed to download "a track by a guy I don't remember, who's Larry's nephew, and burned the track on a CD. We then had two CD players hooked up (for a sound check)."

There remained one test. Ramone, a veteran producer, would give the aural equivalent of the sniff test.

"We had the computer hooked up and the CD player hooked up through very high-quality speakers, and played it," said Kearby. "Phil had known this was coming forever. But it's one thing to know it's coming. It's another to actually see it work."

Ramone listened to the original track, then the one just downloaded and burned onto a CD. He looked up at the assembled executives eager for his stamp of approval.

"Oh, this is going to piss off a lot of people," he said.

*   *   *

The new system, termed e_mod fueled by Liquid Audio in a power-play by the N2K executives, wasn't an overnight sensation with the public.

No one, not even N2K or Liquid Audio, expected much of an immediate economic impact from the sale of downloads. Both adamantly refused to reveal the number of actual downloads, but admitted most came from curious record industryites.

"I don't think it's going to change the record industry in the next day or two," said N2K's Larry Rosen in the days immediately following e_mod's launch. "Where we are is proof of concept, that this is a technology that's showing a completely new way to distribute music and along with it, a whole new concept of how music could be delivered."

But not everyone in the record industry was excited, Rosen noted.

"There's always the status quo players, especially people who are in leadership positions," he said. "If this is the system that works at this time and I'm a leader in that particular space, usually it also means I have a lot invested in that space. I wish things just stay the same way. But in reality, you see this giant kind of sea change taking place here. So the people who get it and get on with it

move forward in these areas. The people who don't probably try to resist and probably get trampled in this thing."

      *   *   *

The birth of the digital downloading world was followed by another revolutionary move. The Artist
Formerly Known As Prince became the first musician to
attempt to break the economic slavery of the record store,
initially announcing that his albums would be available
only via the Internet or an 800 number, beginning with his
next, "Crystal Ball."

The move to the Net was not surprising, given
TAFKAP's antipathy toward the traditional system, best
demonstrated by his writing the word "Slave" on his
cheek during the latter stages of his distribution through
Warner Bros. Records, a Time Warner-owned record label.

The "Crystal Ball" package was issued in a a clear,
round case without the traditional CD booklet or track
listing. Fans seeking the notes were instead referred to a
web site for a complicated process of saving and printing
files, a process many found cumbersome.

The plan to circumvent traditional distribution
methods for music was to take orders for "Crystal Ball"
and start manufacturing when 100,000 orders were
received, the claimed financial break-even point for the
album. Fans were encouraged to order via Prince's web
site (www.love4oneanother) or to call 1-800-Newfunk.

But taking orders and fulfilling them turned out to
be a larger problem than the Artist's system was set up to
handle.

What was expected to be an album released just a
few months from the initial August, 1997 announcement
stretched to February 1998, angering some customers.

As a result, a confusing web developed, one that
underlined the problems of building a distribution system
from scratch.

TAFKAP originally announced that he was taking

orders for a limited-edition, three-CD set of his music titled "Crystal Ball," which would include new music and previously bootlegged material. He later announced that he would add to the package a disc of acoustic music with some overdubbing, titling that work "The Truth."

"The Artist never wanted to have a wide release on "Crystal Ball," because for the most part, it represented previously bootlegged material that was leaked by pirate infringers of his throughout the years," said Londell McMillan, a "friend and counselor" to the Artist. "So what he decided he wanted to do was to make a clean version of some bootleg material and would make it a limited kind of collector's CD of music."

The initial run was originally 250,000 pieces, McMillan said. "And we sold that. We sold it out."

Once that limit was reached, McMillan said, "a number of calls came in through our 1-800 line that there was a large demand for the product from people who weren't able to access it through the Internet. So we decided to supply the top three retailers that purchased the most amount of his product for his last CD, which at the time was "Emancipation."

Best Buy, Blockbuster, and Musicland were selected for a very untraditional one-way sale of this new version of "Crystal Ball." "He (TAFKAP) sold the product to those retailers, who in turn sold the product to various different retailers," McMillan said.

But fans were still waiting for the "Crystal Ball" set they had ordered over the Internet to arrive, and weren't getting satisfactory answers from NPG Records when they attempted to contact them, complaining of constantly ringing phones that weren't answered, indifferent responses when they did reach someone, and multiple attempts to cancel orders being ignored.

The delay in obtaining music from their favorite artist was frustrating enough. But when the four-CD retail version of "Crystal Ball" appeared in February 1998 in stores, it was priced at roughly half of the $50-plus-$10 handling Internet price at some locations. Worse, some fans saw it in stores before their alleged limited edition set had arrived at their homes.

"They're so disorganized, it seems like they're taking the orders and cancellations and writing them down on scraps of paper," said fan Chris Coleman, 31, of Bolivar, Tennessee, who tried to cancel his Internet order without success and then turned the matter over to his credit card company. "I've heard that story more than one time."

Roger Friedman of New York, a freelance writer, said he posted a column to Microsoft's "Cinemania" site about his negative experiences with "Crystal Ball," which arrived at his home in June after he placed an order in January. "No note, no apology," he said. "I had a lot of people e-mail me saying this happened to them also. I know the whole idea was to buck the system, but it hasn't worked."

To mollify fans, another disc was later added to the Internet package, the 11-song suite "Kamasutra," bringing the Internet package ultimately to a five-CD set. Fans were also given a t-shirt to ease the pain of waiting.

McMillan explained the problem as one of confusion and overwhelming demand.

"One thing that was important initially that did push back the fulfillment on two occasions was that the demand was overwhelming for NPG Records, " McMillan said. "They thought there was just going to be a release and it was going to be something that was kind of a limited set. But once the orders started coming in, it became an issue of "Wow! You really have to fulfill these orders."

It was not just a matter of taking orders and putting out records, McMillan said. "You have to actually manufacture the records, package the records, do the artwork, get everything coordinated, do the credit checks, do all that kind of stuff. So it was, you know, some of the growing pains of new technology and alternative distribution methods."

There was also confusion as to the nature of the Internet package versus what later appeared in retail, McMillan said.

"Many people who ordered it over the Internet had to wait until the actual product was available, and after we sold out all of our Internet product, we had arrangements with three of the retailers to go direct to retail with a four-CD version as opposed to a five-CD version of the same product," McMillan said. "But they were two different types of packages around some of the same music."

Some of the delays for shipping came from transaction problems, McMillan said. "Many of the Internet subscribers, they didn't pay their COD. And some of them weren't approved. They put a credit card down and once it was processed – because we have a processing application – it wasn't approved."

Although the initial run of Crystal Ball sold out, the embarrassment caused by the shipping problems made many artists and executives think twice about similar attempts at going it alone.

Still, said Marc Geiger, the CEO of Internet site ARTISTdirect, even with the problems, "he still got 83,000 orders on a $50 box set, which is pretty damn good."

That wasn't enough for TAFKAP to continue to go it alone. In 1999, he licensed "Rave Un2 The Joy Fantastic" to Arista for international distribution.

The Internet experiment by the Artist was noteworthy, even if it didn't spawn a wave of immediate imitators. Artists were beginning to become aware that there were alternatives to the traditional path of signing a recording deal and then awaiting instructions from the home office.

Larry Rosen of N2K reported in 1997 that he was

negotiating with some artists on major labels who were at the end of their contracts regarding Internet distribution, as well as some veterans currently without a recording home.

While artists were talking, other Internet companies were actively working to enlist record companies in the digital revolution.

     *   *   *

Early in their existence, both Liquid Audio and a2b Music were working hard to recruit labels.

They didn't meet much enthusiasm.

"For years I had known that the record industry is not technology bent," said Liquid Audio's Gerry Kearby. "They had largely disassociated themselves from owning recording studios. Primarily they don't own technology. So we got that message over again as we tried to get them to think about buying servers. They said, "Look, can't we out-source this stuff?"

As both Liquid and a2b began to shift into hosting scattered events for the ever-skittish record labels, a new constituency raised some objections, ones which were heard in the record label offices since they came from its primary customers: retailers.

The record stores of the nation were watching the digital distribution revolution and getting very nervous. For all the danger downloadable music posed to record labels, the middle-man was even more vulnerable to being disintermediated, an Internet-speak buzz word for shoved aside.

Both Liquid and a2b began to bend over to accommodate the complainers.

"I would much rather be viewed as a firm that has value-added services that can help a retailer, whether it's a local record store or a large national chain or pure play Internet retailer, than be viewed as a barbarian at the gate," said Miller.

His company was particularly anxious to involve both retail and record labels, hoping that such an alliance would ease the a2b path in becoming the predominant downloading format. Experiments with making digital products available through retail were an integral part of the early a2b strategy.

Liquid Audio was also working hard to get retail support.

"We began to talk to a lot of retailers who said, "We do want to have digital downloads someday. We've got to have the digital downloads integrated into our store, into our shopping carts," said Kearby. "But we don't want to own the storage. And neither did the record industry want these guys to really have these digital masters."

Liquid Audio's solution was RIFs, the remote inventory fulfillment system. RIFs allowed digital music to exist on the Liquid Audio server under secure control to be integrated into the e-commerce environment of an e-retailer.

Yet both of those cooperative efforts were soon going to be put to a severe test by one of the record industry's biggest acts.

Brickbats and Mortar

In September of 1997, Capitol Records had what it thought was a great idea: explore the world of new media by offering Duran Duran fans a new digitally downloadable single and an Internet-only remix of that single.

The idea was groundbreaking. The press release announcing the download thumped its chest, saying the Duran Duran promotion was "signaling a new era in Internet music promotion and a step forward for music commerce."

But instead of cheers, the result of the promotion was a lot of angry retailers and a setback for the larger mission of getting major record label music online.

The single "Electric Barbarella," part of Duran Duran's "Medazzaland" album due out that October, was made available a month before from the Capitol Records web site, http://hollywoodandvine.com. Fans used a Liquid Audio player to purchase the single's standard version for 99 cents, and could also get a longer, Internet-only remix for $1.99.

"It started with us and our management," said Duran Duran keyboardist Nick Rhodes. "We'd been talking about it for a very long time. We'd be waiting for the right opportunity to come along to be able to download and sell music through the Internet."

At first, the concept "met with considerable resistance from Capitol Records," said Rhodes. "But much to their credit, they did finally come around and realize the potential."

The objections weren't necessarily focused on the particular issue of selling a single.

"As with a lot of new technologies, it's fear, more than anything else, and politics," Rhodes said. "They didn't broach this, but it does put into question the necessity of record companies, particularly for a lot of smaller acts. If they are able to access this technology, it will be much easier for them to sell their own product directly."

Lou Mann, senior VP of Capitol Records sales, probably wished he wasn't in the record business when he had to deal with the fallout from retailers.

"They reacted.....how do I say this?" said Mann in the days following the promotion. "A few of the retailers were very concerned, primarily because it wasn't completely, fully explained to them, and saw this as us being in competition with them."

The sticking point was that something was available on the Internet prior to its appearance on the store shelves, something that would likely remind the consumer that record stores, like record companies, were also an endangered species in the brand new world of Internet music.

Despite reminders that the biggest obstacle facing most new albums is making the fan base aware that it's on the shelves, thus driving them into the stores, the brick and mortar crowd was skeptical.

Mann tried to put a happy face on the situation. "When we got to them and we explained that this was something done to create awareness of Duran Duran, then they understood and were fine about it," he said. "The other thing they were concerned about is that this was available on the Net prior to retail. That was a really strong point."

So strong that many retailers threatened not to carry the album in their stores at all if Duran Duran released the single on the Net prior to its appearance on store shelves.

Capitol finally caved in to the hostility. "We basically altered our promotion so it was consistent with their timetable," Mann said, making the single simultaneous with retail's release.

"Everyone is worried about this giant threat," said Mann, who later joined the new media world as head of New Media Properties at the House of Blues. "Is this really a threat to the future of retail? We'll be able to share information with these retailers as to how many specifically downloaded, 200 or 20,000. No one else is able to share information with them to see if it's truly a threat or merely a beep on the radar."

The truth, though, was obvious to everyone. "I think that there's no question that digital downloading five years from now, the whole universe will change," Mann said. "We're really aware of that. The cold numbers, we don't know that."

In fact, although the Duran Duran incident was the most prominent shot across the bow of retail, record companies were already quietly selling CDs on their individual sites. Sony and Warner Bros. were among the early pioneers, offering a mix of hits and catalog.

The record industry was downplaying its experiment. "Nobody goes, "Oh, I want to buy Madonna, so I guess I'll go to the Warner Bros. site," said Hilary Rosen,

CEO of the RIAA, during a chat on 1997 sales. "People don't think that way."

    *   *   *

Emboldened by the rising Net wave, artists were increasingly striking out for new territory.

One of the earliest was Todd Rundgren, whose early '70s hits "Hello, It's Me" and "We Got To Get You A Woman" were later eclipsed by his pioneering work in multimedia.

Rundgren announced in 1997 that he would soon make his work available via a subscription service available to anyone with Internet access.

The service, dubbed "PatroNet," would allow fans to dial into Rundgren's Net site (http://www.waking-dreams.com) to receive song tracks, participate in chats with the artist, and receive updates on potential artwork to accompany the finished product. Subscriptions would last as long as it took Rundgren to complete each album.

"The advantage is that electronic distribution and subscription underwriting of the production allows a greater number of artists to survive on smaller audiences," he said.

"It's been a pattern for many years that when a record of mine gets released, a hardcore audience goes out and buys it right away," said Rundgren. "So in reality, the production of the record is being underwritten by the same people every time. Why not eliminate the middleman now that the Web and this kind of connectivity makes it possible to communicate point to point with these people?"

Rundgren had a 20-year deal with Warner Bros. Records that ended in the early 1990s. He then experimented with multimedia music, releasing "No World Order" on CD-ROM and CD-I in 1993, and an Enhanced CD, "The Individualist," in 1995.

Convention wasn't totally abandoned under

Bob Kohn, cofounder of digital downloading site EMusic.com *(formerly GoodNoise)*, made a key speech at the RIAA/Diamond Multimedia trial on the Rio portable player. *(credit: Dawn Laureen)*

Nick Turner was a cyberspace pioneer, founding the Rocktropolis site and managing Sky Cries Mary, the first band featured on an Internet webcast. *(credit: Dawn Laureen)*

Ted Cohen was an early mover in multimedia as a Philips Electronics executive. He later became one of L.A.'s most prominent Internet consultants.
(credit: Dawn Laureen)

Marc Geiger co-founded ARTISTdirect, a web network for major artists and home to the Ultimate Band List.
(credit: Dawn Laureen)

Hilary Rosen, CEO of the Recording Industry Association of America, the record industry's point person in the digital music revolution.
(credit: Mary Noble Ours)

Cary Sherman, general counsel to the Recording Industry Association of America, was the chief patrolman on the information superhighway.
(credit: Mary Noble Ours)

Michael Robertson (l), chairman of MP3.com, and Bob Kohn (r), co-founder of EMusic.com, were the traditional record industry's most outspoken opponents.
(credit: Dawn Laureen)

Rob Lord (l) and Jeff Patterson (r), co-founders of the Internet Underground Music Archive, the first big digital music site. Early in its existence, Lord and Patterson used the University of California at Santa Cruz's computer lab to digitize images for their site. They didn't own a scanner.

(credit: Chris Davis)

An early IUMA site design.

(credit: Chris Davis)

Ground zero for the digital music revolution: Jeff Patterson's bedroom, where the first songs were uploaded early in 1994.

(credit: Jeff Patterson)

Todd Rundgren was the first artist to offer fans a subscription to his music, art, and other musings over the Internet.

(credit: Dawn Laureen)

A four-time Grammy nominee, Thomas Dolby Robertson used his knowledge of computer music to start Beatnik, an interactive music company. Dolby won Yahoo! Internet Life's Lifetime Achievement in Internet Music in 1998.

(credit: Dawn Laureen)

David Bowie's free digital down-load of "Telling Lies" was one of the biggest events in the early stages of Internet music. He later became one of the first artists to offer his entire album via digital download.

(credit: Dawn Laureen)

Michael Robertson, chairman of MP3.com, spent much of 1998 and 1999 on the road, speaking at conventions and panels. He used the forums to point out the tradi-tional record industry's problems, a tactic that won him few friends among the establishment.

(credit: Dawn Laureen)

Billy Idol tried to give an MP3 Christmas gift to his fans. His record company had other ideas.
(credit: Dawn Laureen)

At AT&T's a2b Music, chief operating officer Larry Miller helped break new ground in digital music distribution before moving to Reciprocal, a digital rights management firm.
(credit: Tess Taylor)

Some of the leaders in digital music gathered for a panel sponsored by the Los Angeles Music Network. Shown, L-R, are Steve Rennie, ARTISTdirect; Jim Griffin, OneHouse; Tess Taylor, LAMN president; Thomas Dolby Robertson, musician/CEO of Beatnik; and Wendy Hafner, Intel Corp. director of music marketing.
(credit: Dawn Laureen)

Gerry Kearby brought a background that included stints as a drummer, sound engineer, entrepreneur, and audio expert to his job as CEO of digital music pioneer Liquid Audio. *(credit: Chris Randall)*

Jim Griffin was one of digital music's visionaries, setting the agenda for countless artists, labels, and related businesses. *(credit: Dawn Laureen)*

Chuck D was one of the first artists to speak out on the Internet's potential to challenge the established record industry. *(credit: Michael Angelo Chester)*

PatroNet. Packaged discs of finished albums were still available in stores at regular CD prices, with online subscribers able to obtain a hard copy for the manufacturing cost.

But Rundgren was banking that there would be enough people willing to pay between $20-$30 for the privilege of hearing his work as it was actually being produced.

"Once a month they might get a little e-mail notice that there's a new tune and that they can go to a special site and download a copy of the tune to their machine," he said, adding that he expected his productivity and creativity to be enhanced by the new process.

"You don't have to be so precious about everything because it's not going through that long and expensive manufacturing process of being enshrined on a plastic disc."

Thomas Dolby, best known for his quirky hit single "She Blinded Me With Science" in the early '80s, was another multimedia pioneer with an aversion to plastic discs.

Dolby, who founded his own company to develop professional audio tools and technologies geared toward the Internet (first called "Headspace," and later changed to Beatnik Inc.) launched a web site devoted to his own music in 1995, saying packaged media would be "left in the dust" by the Internet's growth.

With CD-ROMs and other packaged media, "you commit a minimum of a year and millions of dollars to fill up 50 megabytes of content without knowing if anyone is interested," Dolby said. "Online, you can stick something up quickly and get feedback quickly. If you're wrong, you can do a U-turn.

Dolby was looking to the Net even at that early stage as a platform for his music. "Primarily as a creative person rather than a businessman, it appeals to me to try to make a business out of doing stuff on the Internet rather than have it shrink-wrapped and put on the shelves," he said. "For the artist, that's fantastic. I don't have to write songs and package them into 12 slots. If I write a couple tonight, I can have them online and get feedback by morning. That's an instant form of gratification."

But most important, such activity was a form of...well, self-gratification.

"In the process, we've cut out (record executives), radio programming and retailers," said Dolby "It may be a smaller market, but I'll keep all the revenue."

*   *   *

At the same time Rundgren and Dolby had, at least mentally, taken a step away from physical CDs toward digital music, so did the major record industry.

The problem was that Rundgren and Dolby were doing so voluntarily. The record industry was being dragged into it, like it or not.

MP3 was spreading like a virus across the Net by the Fall of 1997. The college campuses were picking up on it, racing to become the first to break a single, much in the manner of radio stations.

In November of 1997, clips from U2's forthcoming album "Pop" began to circulate on the Net, causing Island Records to warn radio stations and Internet sites that broadcasting the sound clips constituted infringement on its copyrights. The appearance of the clips marked one of the first times a major act had its release date broken by the Net.

The two 30-second clips from the U2 album, "Discotheque," the album's first single, and "Wake Up, Dead Man," also surfaced at radio and television outlets ambitious enough to head to the Net for a listen.

Although at first the clips were reported to have been obtained by hackers who managed to break into the group's recording studio via a camera sending pictures of the recording process over the Internet – an absurd allegation on its face – it later turned out that the sounds were culled from a promo video sent to Pacific Rim countries to tout the upcoming album and an anticipated tour.

A U2 spokesman later confirmed that the origin of the Net-flurry was a Hungarian fan who had obtained a promotional tape and translated it to the Net. His handiwork was then copied by others.

The tipoff that the clips didn't come from the studio was the quality of the sound bytes. The audio was termed "incomplete and degraded" versions of the songs by Island, both problems not usually associated with digitally-obtained copies.

In December, 1998, Syracuse University student Josh Wardell was one of the first U.S. college students to gain notoriety from his Net activities.

Wardell, taping an early broadcast of cuts from Pearl Jam's album "Yield" from Syracuse modern rock radio station WKRL, immediately posted the songs "In Hiding," "Lowlight" and "Pilate" to his fan web site, where it was available to any and all Pearl Jam fanatics.

But Wardell wasn't the only fan on the march. By January of 1998, new music from such superstars as Van Halen, Metallica, Eric Clapton, and Madonna had been posted on the Internet before its official release in the U.S.

The first single from the new Madonna album, "Ray of Light," popped up on several Internet sites weeks before its official release date.

"Frozen" was released on Jan. 23, 1998 to radio stations in several foreign markets, which quickly resulted in the creation of at least two Internet sites offering the song free to anyone who wished to download it.

The plan for "Ray of Light" was to have it released in several foreign markets on Feb. 13. USA radio stations got "Frozen" Feb. 14, with the album to follow on March 3.

Bob Merlis, a spokesman for Madonna's Warner Bros. Records, said at the time that the company would try to squelch "with any means at our disposal" any sites that offered free downloadable files of Warner Bros. material, "whether it's a Madonna song or a Doobie Bros. song out for 25 years."

However, Internet sites that offered songs for listening only – so-called streaming media – were okay, Merlis said, so long as the song has been "legitimately released" by the company. "We consider that the equivalent of radio."

But, Merlis added, "what I said about streaming does not hold for stuff we haven't released. If the song hasn't been released in (the U.S.) market, we will go after them."

Some artists didn't care.

Jay Kay of Jamiroquai was non-plussed by any music appearing on the Web.

"If people want to put things up and we share the same philosophies and basic ideals, I don't see anything wrong with that, because, you know, Jamiroquai is one of those things that people just share, you know? It's there for everybody to sort of be inspired by. So if people are inspired by it, I don't know, do whatever they want to do. Then that's fine. I don't mind."

Others did.

"I don't think it's out of control yet," said Mike Simpson, half of the Dust Brothers production team that worked with Beck, the Rolling Stones and Beastie Boys, among others. "But I think the potential is there. I mean, I've heard rumors that you can now compress an entire album's worth of material into two megabytes and basically e-mail records to your friends. That's potentially scary because it really strips away all the (copyright) protection that's been set up."

Those charged with enforcing copyright protections

were no less worried.

"I have no illusions that I can control this," said RIAA CEO Hilary Rosen. "The best we can do is to set as many good enforcement precedents as we can and do as much education as we can. And ultimately, technology is going to have to solve this problem better than we can the way we're doing it."

In early 1998, the RIAA obtained judgments against three unnamed Internet pirates in Federal court, accusing them of posting sound files from hundreds of recording artists, allowing anyone free downloads. The judgments were the first in the U.S. against Internet recording copyright infringers. Although victorious, the organization decided to use the case more as a warning. As part of the settlement, the RIAA agreed not to collect fines totaling well over $1 million per violation from the offenders, provided they agreed not to post music again.

At that moment, the RIAA claimed 30-40% of its anti-piracy efforts were being spent online, up from 5% the year before.

"We could triple our budget tomorrow on this and there would still be more to do," said Rosen. "Every day we shut down sites with hundreds of recordings. The thing that makes the Pearl Jam and Madonna and last week Van Halen and Eric Clapton unique is that that's material that hasn't been released yet. Popping a release date or getting an advance tape was always a hot thing to do. But it was always fairly an insider game. Now, one insider can distribute it to thousands instantly. It changes the drama of it, I think, not to mention the potential harm."

But even those worried about copyright protection sensed that something wasn't quite right about the hoopla surrounding piracy

"Here's one of the things that I have kind of been thinking," said Dust Brother Mike Simpson. "Perhaps the record industry is more on top of this issue than they're letting on. Right now, they're so reliant on retail that they have to be careful not to alienate retail by letting them know that they're going full-bore into digital delivery systems. I think they don't want to undermine the system themselves before they've got their systems in place, so they may be playing down the fact that they really are concentrating on this."

As for his fellow artists, Simpson said, a lot of new acts "are really excited about the prospect of not having to work for The Man anymore."

*   *   *

While it appeared on the surface that the MP3 piracy problem was spiraling out of control, others were taking action.

Jim Griffin of Geffen Records was monitoring the activity on the web and engaging the young MP3 fans he encountered.

One President's Day weekend, Griffin decided to try an experiment. Locating a master directory on the Net of MP3 sites, he took note of any site that contained full-length songs from Geffen artists that Griffin claimed had complained about infringing materials on the Net. He then e-mailed each site that had posted a contact e-mail address or phone number. If none was available, the Internet service provider was contacted.

"What we did was just send them a polite note, reminding them that we were available to ask permission," said Griffin. "Our policy at Geffen was to engage people, not ignore them."

The legal department of Geffen had warned Griffin that if he encountered a file site, he could not ignore it. If the server log showed that Geffen was aware of the infringement but didn't take action, it would potentially counter the company's copyright infringement arguments.

"I think that it was actually good for all because it

created a dialogue," said Griffin of his actions. "In other words, until that point, the groups had been off in two different corners, not even communicating, and the industry was basically pretending that nothing could be done about it. I think that it compelled a dialogue. It was not our intention to shut down anybody's web site."

Some in the MP3 community begged to differ immediately after Griffin's action, which marked him in some quarters as a tool of the establishment. For a short time, he became something of a bogeyman on some boards.

However, the somewhat hands-off attitude, which didn't stalk the infringers so much as point out the error of their ways, was in keeping with the spirit of the MP3 community, most of whom were ardent fans of their music postings and champions of the respective artists.

Chris Nelson, a writer for SonicNet's Addicted to Noise, covered some of the MP3 community's activities in his duties for the online news service.

Nelson said his subjects posted songs because "they think it generates interest in the album. If people started putting up clips, however they came upon them, whether they taped them off the radio or got them through industry leaks or whatever, and the general opinion in the Pearl Jam fan community was that they were god-awful, I wouldn't think that they would leave them up."

The fans would not forego a purchase, Nelson contended. Almost all of them, "maybe to a one," Nelson said, would buy the album. "In fact, several have told me that they only intended to keep the "Yield" files up until the album went on sale. And as soon as it went on sale, they would remove them, because they didn't want to hurt album sales."

Kevin O'Connor, a 19-year Williams College student, was one of the fans with a Pearl Jam site at the time of the "Yield" release. Although he didn't post any songs pre-release, he believes that no harm was done by anyone posting a low-quality clip.

"The web can be a real advantage to a band such as Pearl Jam in that you're going to get tons of exposure, people aren't going to have to buy your music to hear it, and what they're going to hear may interest them enough so that maybe you'll think about buying the CD," O'Connor said. But man, even if you like the music, you're not going to want to keep that little clip of poor-quality music, because it's just not going to be good enough for you. You're going to want to buy the CD at that point."

Ironically, the people who probably cared the least about the incident was the band. Like many acts, including the Grateful Dead, Phish, and the Black Crowes, Pearl Jam allows its fans to trade copies of its material if they don't profit from the transaction.

*   *   *

While the industry was getting its battle plans together, Michael Robertson began forming the business plan for MP3.com.

The beginnings weren't grand. Robertson worked out of a bedroom in his home.

"The guys in the company all had cable modems, because San Diego is the cable modem capital of the world," recalled Robertson. "And we just put our phones on speaker phone so you had a virtual office. You were talking to the guy part of the day or whatever."

Robertson, having seen the traffic in MP3 files on the Internet, was ready to attempt to commercialize that activity. He had his chief salesman compile a list of the ten top MP3 sites in the world. "Make sure they're all legal and we'll just try to buy one," he said.

Meanwhile, Robertson himself attempted to secure the domain name MP3.com. It was already in use, so Robertson sent the owner, Martin Paul, an e-mail inquiring about its availability.

Paul sent back an odd reply. "What's MP3?"

"I'm thinking, "domain names don't fall out of the sky, buddy,"Robertson recalled. "You had to register it. Why did you register it if you don't know what MP3 is?"

The answer was a simple accident of fate. When Paul had registered his domain with Internic, the organization charged with registering and cataloging the Internet's domain names, he (like anyone registering a domain) received a code name establishing a bonafide identity for future contact with the organization.

"It's usually your initials plus a number if somebody else already has your initials," Robertson said.

Martin Paul received the code name MP3 from Internic. "And he was in the mood to register a domain name, so he said, "Well, I'm a computer geek, so I'll register the domain name of my Internic handle," said Robertson. "Which is a pretty odd thing to do, really."

Paul wasn't sure what he would do with the MP3 domain name, but was definitely interested in the $1000 Robertson offered him for the rights. Robertson sent him a check, and the deal was concluded.

Today, when domain names are sold for hundreds of thousands of dollars by early prospectors, the value of such titles are clear.

But in mid-1997, many saw such transactions as the equivalent of vanity license plates. Among them, Robertson's wife, still reeling from the financial fallout of his previous failed business venture.

I said, "Hey, you know, I bought a domain name today," Robertson told his wife.

"What'd you buy?"

I said, "I bought something called MP3.com."

"What'd you pay for it?"

I said, "$1000."

She said, "Are you out of your mind? What is MP3?"

Robertson, who is still married as of this book's printing, next discovered a site called MP3 Shopping Mall, run by a resident of the Netherlands. The site specialized in listing software programs rather than illegal songs, Robertson said.

Another e-mail by Robertson offered $2500 for the web site's content and $500 per month to become the web master.

"I'm not even sure how old this guy was," said Robertson. "My guess was he's pretty young because he was doing it for fun, no advertising or anything. So we took his list of software programs and we put it behind the MP3.com domain name, and that was our web site."

Robertson debuted the site on a crisp Fall morning in October, 1997, activating it at 10 a.m. Pacific time.

At 2:00 in the afternoon he received his first call from a potential advertiser.

"That's pretty surprising," Robertson said. "Because usually advertisers don't call you. You have to call them. So we said, "Hmmm."

At the end of that first day, without any registration on search engines or prior advertising, MP3.com had 10,000 visitors to the web site. "You don't have to be a really smart guy to figure out that I went home and said, "There's something here," Robertson said.

But Robertson was now faced with developing a site that would return those visitors over and over. Most had likely stopped by MP3.com in hopes of snagging some music.

MP3.com had no music content and no music connections.

"We didn't know anyone. We didn't even know like one person in a band," said Robertson. "We knew nothing."

Actually, it wasn't only a matter of business connections. Robertson was truly focused on the Net and tech matters, to the virtual exclusion of music, claims one early observer.

"I remember the first time I went down to MP3.com, which was the second bedroom upstairs in his house," says the source. "And what really struck me when I was looking around was, where's the stereo? And then I thought, "Where are the CDs?"

"I said, 'Michael, where are your CDs?' He goes, "'Huh, what? Oh, I don't have that many. Actually, my wife has six.' And he freely admits that. He's not a music guy."

At first, the workaround devised to overcome the lack of audio content was to aggregate news articles on MP3, clearly a rising area of interest on the Net.

There was just one problem. There were few news articles on MP3 in late 1997.

At the time, MP3.com had four employees: two engineers, a salesman, and Robertson. They all turned and looked at Robertson. He was elected to write what soon became one of the music industry's hottest forums.

"I had to learn about the music industry," said Robertson. "I'd been on the Net for a very long time, and knew it fairly well, from who's running different companies and relationships, all that kind of stuff. But this is the music industry, and the music industry is incredibly complex."

So Robertson embarked on what he termed "a personal crusade" to learn about the music business. The MP3.com site bears testament to his diligence. The first hundred articles, still archived, all bear his byline. "People looked at that and they thought, "Well, a nugget of wisdom has fallen out of Michael's head," when actually, what was happening was that I was learning something," Robertson said. "And every week, I'd learn two new things and I'd write an article about that."

Robertson was doing his homework at Net speed. His days were filled with talking to players in the emerging Net music market, interacting with music business

91

people, interviewing, reading, and writing.

"If you look through the news archives from the oldest to the youngest, you'll see Michael learning as he goes along," said Robertson. "When I started, I didn't know what publishing rights were. No clue."

But there was one highly disturbing fact that Robertson kept uncovering in all his research. "Of course, as I learned, I realized that, my God, this music industry is (a) really complex and (b) artists take the shaft. There's a lot of hurdles for an artist in the process."

Clearly, there was an opportunity. But Robertson, for all his research, was still far outside the record industry loop of attorneys, A&R talent scouts, and club owners. How could he link his site with that network?

The answer, of course, was the Internet.

"We have to get content," said Robertson. "But we have this problem – we didn't have money to buy content. We didn't know anyone who had content. And we didn't make our own content. So what were we going to do? So we started off scouring the net, looking for any bands, anywhere, that were putting up MP3 files. And we would simply link to them."

The first bands to come aboard MP3.com included two jazz bands, a blues artist and one alternative act.

But hosting the files on other sites was cumbersome, Robertson claimed. Soon, the idea morphed from linking to creating a service for the bands, fulfilling Robertson's original goal of devising a service model that could be scaled to any degree.

Thus, MP3.com became a web service that hosted music, collecting data and then producing web pages.

There was one difference between MP3.com and a record company – MP3.com wasn't asking for ownership of the master recordings for eternity.

Instead of the traditional record industry deal, where artists forfeited ownership of their master recordings and agreed to long-term deals with the same employer, MP3.com allowed at-will termination in return for licensing rights.

"We needed to make no barriers between us and the content," said Robertson. "So that's why we said, "Hey, it's non-exclusive. Just cause you work with us doesn't mean you can't work with anyone else. We wanted to make it as artist-friendly as we could to attract that content. Cause we knew that hey, if we attract content, then that will attract visitors, which is, of course, something that grows and snowballs on itself."

The MP3.com deal required artists to donate at least one full-length promotional song for digital downloading.

In return, the artist received their own web site design and hosting package, plus back-end functions on shipping and packaging. The act also received daily data on which songs were being listened to, which songs were being downloaded, and the number of CDs sold. Functions were added to the site on a continuing basis, including personalized radio stations for the bands and the ability for visitors to compile playlists.

"The most famous thing people have to say about us is they've got 10,000 nobodies," Robertson said. "Actually, that's what's helped us, because we've been listening to those artists that come to us and say this is what I want. And we've tried to give it to them."

Not everyone was buying into that theory.

"I've always thought that Michael Robertson's a very smart guy who I had a difficult time liking because, to me, he felt like (conservative radio personality) Rush Limbaugh," said Gerry Kearby, CEO of Liquid Audio, which would develop into an archrival of MP3.com.

"I've always suspected that if Rush Limbaugh could make more money being a liberal than a conservative, he would be one," Kearby continued. "He's just too fanatical. And Michael Robertson strikes me that way. I believe that his whole thing is about building up a big old brand, selling it off to Yahoo! or somebody, and that musicians are the fodder. I don't think that he has any particular difference between him and the guys in the record industry that he assails as people who don't care about the artist. That's my fundamental problem with him."

Kearby's vitriol focused on Robertson's greatest talent. Far more than his innovative approach to music aggregation on the Net, more than the actual services he provided, and certainly more than his innate knack for seizing opportunity, Robertson's greatest gift was an utter lack of fear when it came to speaking truth to power.

It was a talent that would make him public enemy No. 1 in the music industry for the first two years of MP3.com's existence.

Law and Disorder

The MP3 movement, though finally gaining attention in the record community, was still relatively underground and directionless in the first half of 1998.

Michael Robertson of MP3.com realized early on that his company needed to become the Yahoo! of music, a new, upstart portal that would galvanize and unite all of the activity in the sector.

One of the people Robertson turned to for advice in his early explorations of the music business was John Parres, whose record industry background spanned A&R work, artist management, and technology consulting.

Parres, one of the earliest advocates of digital music (and later instrumental in bringing Hollywood Records act Alien Fashion Show to MP3.com, the first major label group to participate in a free digital download on the site), came to Robertson's attention through the e-mail network of digital music advocates.

They quickly developed a rapport, spending many

95

nights talking about the music industry and the boundaries and buttons the MP3 movement was pushing.

"Because Michael had no industry experience or perspective at all, John would be a really strong sounding board that he would always go to to figure out how to take different approaches," said Hal Bringman, who handled publicity for Robertson.

Parres is modest about his contribution.

"If I had done MP3.com, or anybody else in the music community had done MP3.com, they wouldn't have given it the fair shot that it deserved," Parres said, reflecting on that early period in Net music's development.

"I think that MP3.com really needed to be a pure Internet play in the very, very early first year. The change truly needed to come from the outside, and so he was pursuing that course. He had a degree of arrogance in realizing and knowing in his soul that this changed everything."

Despite later assertions by record industry rivals, Robertson truly was horrified by the way artists were traditionally treated under music industry contracts, Parres contends. But he was also concerned that they would wake up and realize the new rules created by the Internet, "throw all their stuff on-line and blow him out of the water," Parres said.

Until, that is, he spent more time talking to record executives. Then, Parres asserted, Robertson realized that their outlook was more focused on protecting the status quo. "They don't even realize that they need to be getting into the game," Parres said, quoting a Robertson conversation. He goes, "That's the least of my worries right now."

Robertson was not a perfect leader. Highly wired on cola and power bars, he had a temper that often manifested itself to co-workers. His sister and co-worker, Michelle, a frequent target, was threatened with firing a dozen times a day during stressful moments.

Coming from an impoverished background, Robertson was driven to the point of obsession at times to overcome his roots.

"He wanted to be bigger than that," said Bringman. "He wanted to defeat that and I think he saw this was his opportunity to prove everybody wrong. I think psychologically, it's part of what drives him. He's so driven to the point that a lot of times, you just can't talk to him, cause he gets into that place. But it's part of that drive, whatever it takes."

From Robertson's conversations with Parres, an idea grew. What if the MP3 community could be gathered for a convention, where all the various elements of the new movement could communicate face-to-face?

"It needed to be a summit, a place where we gather on the mountain to discuss the large issues and try to move things forward in a coordinated and respectful way," Parres recalled of the moment.

The organization of the initial event was haphazard. A public relations coordinator was hired only two weeks before the gathering, a one-day event which was scheduled for San Diego on July 3, 1997.

Initially, the summit was viewed as a way to get a few people together over pizza and beer across a picnic table. Word of mouth and e-mail was the primary organizational tool. If you were in the digital music community, or at least active on its message boards, you were made aware of the gathering and invited to drop in.

Soon, however, the organizers realized that what they were concocting was going to be much bigger and much more significant. The attendees ranged from foreign consumer electronics manufacturers to digital music site webmasters to a lone and brave representative of the Recording Industry Association of America, senior VP for business affairs Steven Marks, who wore a paper bag with eye holes cut out during a panel session, a gimmick to defuse the obvious verbal abuse promised by the session.

Bringman points to the summit as one of the keys to MP3.com's success.

"These different companies and people started talking to one another, having met at the summit, and this organization didn't exist before," said Bringman. "A lot of people that didn't know each other before started talking and forming alliances."

"It definitely had a revolutionary feel. There was definitely a sense of history being made," echoed Parres. "Xing Technologies sponsored a party at the Hyatt Hotel in San Diego the night before. The Germans were in the room, the Koreans were there. That's when I realized it was international."

There was also, Parres admitted, "a high geek factor." Most of the crowd consisted of technology people, mostly engineers and webmasters. Few traditional music industryites bothered to attend.

That may have fueled the undercurrent of the convention, which Parres describe as "a very anti-music industry vibe that was floating through. That was very clear to me. I don't think it was so much everyone felt like artists were getting screwed, but I do know that a lot of those folks on the tech side felt like music was overpriced and out of the reach of too many people, and that this empowered artists and anybody ... it made the music business available to anybody who wanted to get into it."

One such outsider was already making an impact on the MP3 scene. His name was Justin Frankel, the inventor of Winamp, the leading MP3 player.

*   *   *

In 1997, Justin Frankel quit college after two quarters, moving back to the family home in sleepy Sedona, Arizona.

Frankel, a laid-back, dude-speak teenager, didn't

immediately get a full-time job. Instead, he raised enough cash to amuse himself by fixing friends' computers, spending the rest of his time with various hobbies, including computer programming.

In short, Frankel seemed to have no big plans, no real vision, and a somewhat hazy future.

Finally, his parents took action. They told their son that a program he devised to listen to music downloaded from the Internet shouldn't be given away, as he had been doing. Rather, it should be marketed as shareware, an Internet honor system that allows users to try out new software and send a check if they decide to keep it.

The son followed his parent's orders, albeit reluctantly. "I didn't want business stuff to get in the way of a good time," he recalled.

Frankel's shareware program, Winamp, quickly became the most popular player in the world for MP3 sound compression files. "Once I did that and started making some money off it, it was like, 'Whoa,'" says Frankel.

Programming took root early in Frankel's life. An older brother's Atari caught his eye before he was a teenager, but almost anything would have.

"It was just sort of like I had nothing better to do," he said. "Sedona was even smaller than it is now and there wasn't a lot to do. I just started playing around on that and went from there."

Frankel had a vague notion of a career in computer science when he matriculated at the University of Utah. While he soon realized that wasn't what he wanted from life, he did put the college's fast Internet connections to good use.

During one random foray on the Net, he found an MP3 file of the song "Pepper" by the Butthole Surfers, one of his favorite groups. Unfortunately, the player on Frankel's computer – a software that decompresses the sound file and plays it back, akin to a stereo translating a

CD's digital codes – left a lot to be desired.

Despite his laconic personality, Frankel loved creating solutions based on a perceived need. Dissatisfied with the MP3 player he had, he created a new one with better capabilities. "If there's something I think would be useful, then I make it," he said.

He had another talent: the ability to attract people in the digital music and Internet community who would help him grow the company. Frankel hooked up with Tom Pepper, who hosted the Nullsoft servers at his Iowa Internet Service Provider, and Rob Lord, who co-founded IUMA but had moved on to greener pastures.

Another popular Internet software devised by Frankel, SHOUTcast, was borne of a similar need as Winamp. SHOUTcast allows computer users to create their own virtual radio stations, broadcasting MP3 streams taken from compact discs or radio.

Frankel wanted to listen to a radio broadcast on a station in Los Angeles while he was in Arizona. "So basically I started writing software that would let (an L.A. friend) sample his sound card, encode it to MP3, send it out on the Net and send it to me on the fly." Like Winamp before it, SHOUTcast shareware soon took off in popularity.

Winamp had already made Frankel a sort-of celebrity in the world of Internet music. SHOUTcast certified him as one of the true innovators in the field, and soon companies came calling.

"We talked to a lot of people," Frankel said. "But we were still like really psyched about everything we were doing and no one really seemed to have the same level of enthusiasm, so nothing ever really came out of it."

Enter America Online, a company whose populist approach to the Internet causes some technologists to look down their nose. "I had the usual opinion," Frankel said. "I just kept an open mind when we first started talking to them."

Impressed with the company's hands-off approach to operating Internet chat service ICQ after acquiring it, Frankel and his advisers opted to join forces with AOL, which crowed about its coup in landing Frankel. A party in Frankel's honor held in San Francisco was highlighted by a banner proclaiming, "America Online Just Got A Whole Line Cooler."

Yet, just about the time the first word of AOL's approach to Nullsoft filtered out to the Internet music community, another development threatened.

On March 15, 1999, PlayMedia, which created an early MP3 decoding software, claimed Frankel's Winamp was derived from its AMP 0.7 series MP3 decoding engines, developed and copyrighted between 1996 and 1997 and licensed to Justin Frankel in September, 1997 by AMP inventor Tomislav Uzelac. The two companies disagreed over whether the licensed code was still used in Winamp after the agreement ended.

PlayMedia subsequently filed a copyright infringement suit for $20 million, based on the number of allegedly infringing Winamp players distributed by Nullsoft and others containing the "Nitrane" MP3 decoder, most prominently MP3.com.

Early in June, 1999, the suit was settled out-of-court, with Nullsoft agreeing to license some of PlayMedia's MP3 technology for possible use in Winamp players. No other details were released.

Frankel declined to comment on various aspects of the suit, but says, "it was a pretty stupid lawsuit. I can say that. It happens a lot in this country, frivolous lawsuits. I'm just glad it's over with. It was kind of a pain."

That pain was being shared by the record industry when it confronted a new potential threat, webcasting. They turned to an old friend, legislation, to address it.

*   *   *

In 1883, countries from around the world met in

Paris to conceive the first major international treaty designed to protect intellectual property.

The major concern during that period was printed material. But gradually, technological progress added devices and methods of transmitting that property.

By the late 1960s, concerns that sound recordings were being duplicated by unauthorized parties led the World Intellectual Property Organization, the leading international body concerning copyrights, to call for a discussion.

In 1971, WIPO members gathered in Geneva for the awkwardly-titled Convention for the Protection of Producers of Phonograms Against Unauthorized Duplication of Their Phonograms.

There the international body adopted rules governing the reproduction rights of audio recordings. The U.S. soon followed with its own Sound Recording Amendment of 1971, extending U.S. copyright protection to sound recordings for the first time.

But long-time protections for the U.S. broadcasting industry woven into that 1971 law would come back to bite in the digital music age.

The Digital Millenium Copyright Act was passed by the U.S. Congress and signed into law on October, 28, 1998, marking the U.S. implementation of two international treaties, the overall World Intellectual Property Organization Treaty of 1996 and the more specific Performances and Phonograms Treaty.

While DMCA strengthened copyright enforcement for a number of interested parties, including publishers, film studios and record companies, it also created new barriers for Net entrepreneurs who wished to use prerecorded music at a crucial moment in the medium's growth.

Some of the DMCA provisions were understandable. One required Internet Service Providers to take action "expeditiously" against unauthorized postings of copyrighted material once they became aware of same, imposing penalties on them if they did not act. Another said hardware manufacturers could no longer thwart copy-protection schemes in software with their devices.

But one sticky wicket negotiated into the DMCA changed the game for Internet webcasters and clearly put them back under the thumb of record companies at a time when their growing influence offered new hope to weary listeners tired of the same old, highly-controlled terrestrial radio formats.

Instead of being granted the same exemption that radio and television broadcasters had to transmit prerecorded music, webcasters would be governed by a different set of rules.

Record companies, angry that businesses were being built using their content – and overlooking the promotional benefits that they annually spent millions of dollars encouraging radio to apply – requested that webcasters pay both the artists and the record companies.

Terrestrial broadcasters had managed to avoid paying record companies thanks to older laws – and heavy lobbying – but were also allegedly on the hook for Internet simulcasts. (It's worth noting that in their public postures, few planned to obey that provision).

In return for a licensing fee, record companies agreed to grant a statutory blanket license, which would allow webcasters to transmit any prerecorded music without having to contact each and every record company for permission.

While some recording artists stood to gain incrementally from such webcasting fees, the overall impact on their bottom lines was outweighed by the crimp in yet another distribution channel for their music.

The online radio community was most affected by the DMCA. Although they could now obtain more music to broadcast on the Net, the startup businesses, already largely in debt, would now be forced to pony up money to record companies in addition to what they already paid the artists via the American Society of Composers, Authors and Publishers (ASCAP) and Broadcast Music Inc. (BMI).

As of October, 1999, the webcaster fee to record companies had still not been set, but will likely be based on gross revenues of the Internet startups, a particularly hard burden on smaller companies faced with other enormous costs of doing business in the new medium.

In addition to the financial requirements, new restrictions on the particular transmissions of webcasting were put in place. Webcasters couldn't play music by specific artists too often, or more than three songs in a row from the same record. The stations were also required to publish the title of the song and CD being played, and to keep the broadcast non-interactive, meaning personalization features would largely be scrapped. Any broadcast that triggered a recording device was also forbidden.

The Digital Media Association (DiMA), a collection of early movers in the Internet broadcast and content field, including Liquid Audio, RealNetworks, a2b Music and SonicNet, was formed to negotiate with the Recording Industry Association of America on the DMCA webcasting fees. Their relationships were anything but separate. Most of those early movers were already actively working with record companies in various capacities and, it could be argued, eager to exclude less well-funded competitors from the webcasting field.

"Many companies don't have the technology or flexibility to handle this law, and they are really going to fall through the cracks," said David Samuel, CEO of Spinner.com, in a conversation with CNET. Spinner was acquired by America Online in a multimillion dollar deal in June, 1999. "But we are fine with this bill," Samuel added.

The advent of Justin Frankel's SHOUTcast had thrown one further consideration into the mix – almost anyone on the Net could now become a streamer, making it increasingly difficult to track licenses for what could potentially be an infinite number of webcasters.

"One of the central issues during the negotiations on Capitol Hill to enact the new law was jurisdiction," said Jim Griffin. "In other words, who would be at these negotiations? Who would the law cover? Who would it not cover? What if a 14-year old kid shows up with his lawyer and says, "I'm a streamer. I want to be involved."

Griffin said there was always a fear that the 14-year old would show, but it was dismissed as irrational. "Well, (SHOUTcast) is proof that they were right all along," Griffin said. "Any 14-year old kid can stream. And now they're right in the thick of this thing."

＊   ＊   ＊

One of the most popular music sites in the early history of the Net was the Ultimate Band List, which started life in Summer 1994 as a user-driven content site created by California Institute of Technology graduate students Joe Cates and Aurelius Prochazka.

The goal at the time was to assemble music links in one space and have users create their own links, thus creating a one-stop site for artist information. By November of that year, they sold the site to ARTISTdirect, run by music industry veterans Marc Geiger, Don Muller (both instrumental in starting the Lollapalooza tour) and Bill Elson.

But like most World Wide Web sites, the UBL's early incarnation would change drastically as the forces of commerce began to take hold in the medium. In 1998, UBL relaunched itself with a new e-commerce emphasis, adding a link to stores where music and merchandise could be purchased to the site's existing artist biographies, discographies and assorted information.

ARTISTdirect, the parent company of UBL, was also creating separate stores outside the main UBL hub for a number of higher-profile artists. In early 1998, it launched its first venture, creating the official store for the Rolling Stones and over a dozen other acts.

"The biggest hole in the music business was that if you're a consumer, your tickets are bought at a Ticketmaster outlet; sheet music, music books and instruments are bought in another place; used records in another, merchandise at a concert venue," said Marc Geiger, the co-founder and CEO of ARTISTdirect. "If you're a U2 fan or a Pearl Jam fan or a Beastie Boys fan, there's no place you can go to get all the music products by that artist in one place."

Geiger likened the new UBL to stores offering branded merchandise started by Warner Bros. and Disney. "There's no difference between Mickey Mouse and the Rolling Stones," said Geiger. "They're both brands, to an extent."

While the new UBL retained the ability of users to link their band tributes to the site, the goal has clearly shifted from cheerleading to cash. "Most people shop by artist. They don't shop by product type," said Geiger. "All these things are just as valuable as selling the music."

Clearly, the opportunities posed by the online music world were growing. But there were still members of the old guard who didn't want to play that tune.

*   *

The battle lines were clearly being drawn in the industry between those who were wholeheartedly embracing the digital music revolution, and those more inclined to ease into it while protecting the status quo.

By early 1998, Jim Griffin had left his job as head of technology at Geffen Records to form OneHouse, a consulting firm that advised entertainment companies on how to make the transition into the digital medium.

Griffin was not alone in his exodus. Many of the early advocates of digital music had by early 1998 left large record companies or planned to leave, lured away by the chance to innovate outside the boundaries of big corporations.

Those that stayed behind dug in their heels more firmly than ever against what was perceived to be barbarians at the gate, the MP3 music community.

At the time, several strange developments came from people trying to seize the higher ground. A new technology, named MP4, emerged briefly on the scene, serving mostly to confuse the already confused consumers. Other new net music companies popped up on a daily basis, all claiming to offer the newest, the hottest, the grandest digital music experience.

Yet most of the older executives in the record business still clung to the belief that they would be safely retired before digital music had any impact on them.

"There's this difficulty in bringing people up to speed," said one consultant to the record business, asking not to named so as not to spoil his relationships. "It's a little frightening to these guys. Because a lot of them have this theory, especially older guys, that their brains are already wired, the neurons have been connected. And there's this difficulty in trying to grasp this new way of looking at it."

The hardest thing to grasp, the consultant said, was that change was inevitable. Only none of the highly-paid executives dared voice that notion.

"I mean, I understand why they do what they do...who's gonna risk their job? None of them. So the only way that change IS going to occur is if somebody like Michael Robertson stands up and says, "Hey! You guys are wrong!"

Robertson was, by mid-1998, becoming more and more a thorn in the side of the record business. Thanks to

a major front page article in music industry bible
Billboard by Doug Reece (later an MP3.com employee),
the MP3 movement was starting to attract attention from
the mainstream media.

While there were abundant sources willing to discuss the record industry's point of view regarding digital
music, there was no strong counterpoint to their arguments except Robertson. He was a constant presence in
the press, stridently advocating his theory that the record
industry as the world knew it was broken.

But Robertson's chief forum was the message
boards on MP3.com. His "Michael's Minute" became the
bully pulpit for the disenfranchised, the disaffected, and
the discontented, many, if not most, highly involved in the
MP3 community.

"I would find myself every couple hours in the day,
I'd be going back to see what new article or news thing he
had there," said one fan. "He would find any kind of digital news thing that was happening. He was updating. He
helped proliferate the whole thing. He did a lot of that
stuff and I think he always made a really brilliant case."

One of the frequent targets on the board was Liquid
Audio, whose proposal for a secure digital music system
was frequently attacked. In one particularly memorable
moment, Robertson posted a link to a software that would
purportedly crack the encryption of Liquid Audio and
a2b, dubbed a2b2wav.

Gerry Kearby of Liquid Audio called Robertson, and
was disturbed to get a speech rather than an agreement to
take the link down (Kearby denies that the software com-
promised Liquid's encryption).

Miffed at the perceived lack of response, Kearby had
his lawyer send a cease and desist letter to Robertson,
who subsequently took the link down but promptly posted the letter on his site, creating more vitriol in the MP3
community against secure digital music solutions and

fueling the perception that MP3.com was fighting the good fight against the establishment.

Former MP3.com Publicist Hal Bringman remembers the period as galvanizing. A small circle of Robertson confidants would strategize through frequent e-mails and phone calls.

"We'd get up in the morning and get on the phone and figure out new ways to fuck with the RIAA and others," recalled Bringman. "We would always say Liquid Audio had a lame solution that didn't have any users behind it, so they were spending all this money on label people. But they had no users behind them, whereas MP3 had this grassroots support."

Robertson's messages emphasized those real people behind the MP3 movement. "It was part of his strategy to always drive home that it was a real movement, it wasn't something he was hyping," said Bringman. "He just got out in front of it and being the bullhorn for the whole thing."

Robertson was essentially kept at arm's length by the establishment, although there were some feelers about a possible merger of his operation with established recording companies, none of which went anywhere. "There's been a lot of behind-the-scenes, very, very high level conversations going on about how they have got to keep Michael Robertson at a distance and outside the loop," said a source.

Much as those companies were willing to consider embracing him behind closed doors, there was still public antipathy.

In one particular snub, MP3.com claimed it paid to have an ad run in Grammy Magazine, only to have it yanked by the National Academy of Recording Arts and Sciences, which runs the magazine. Robertson posted part of a letter from NARAS on his site in which the organization claimed it was pulling the ad because of the "controversial nature of your product" and limited advertising space, the latter almost unheard of in print publishing.

The battle to ostracize MP3.com reached a head at the Webnoize digital music conference in November of 1998.

MP3.com proudly paraded around the convention wearing t-shirts reading "Who Invited These Guys?" A panel on digital music, featuring Robertson and Kearby, featured some particularly heated exchanges.

After that panel, Dick Wingate, a former PolyGram executive turned Liquid Audio official, came up to a few MP3.com representatives watching the panel from the back of the room.

Veins popping, Wingate had a message for Robertson and his followers: "When MP3 fails, not only will we celebrate, we'll find Michael and step on his throat."

But a lawsuit filed a month earlier by the Recording Industry Association of America would make the failure of MP3 that much more unlikely.

SEVEN

Blame it on Rio

Diamond Multimedia Systems Inc. of San Jose, California described itself as a leader in PC multimedia and Internet connectivity in its corporate handouts.

The Recording Industry Association of America had a different name for it in October, 1998: public enemy number one.

Just one month earlier, Diamond had quietly announced the Rio PMP300, the first portable MP3 player to be sold in the U.S. It followed several overseas devices, including one created by Korean electronics giant Saehan, the Nordic Entertainment MP3Man, introduced in March 1998 and given widespread display at the Jupiter Communications Plug.In digital music conference in July, 1998.

Capable of storing up to 60 minutes of digital music and up to eight hours of voice-quality audio downloaded from the Internet to the PC, the device was smaller than an audio cassette and would not skip. Its list price was $199.

Few paid attention to the initial announcement. One who did was the Recording Industry Association of America, which had been anticipating the U.S. debut of a portable MP3 recording device in the wake of the overseas models over which they had no jurisdiction.

The RIAA began quietly talking to Diamond about the implications of manufacturing a device that would allow music fans to take digitally downloaded songs wherever they wished.

Apparently, they felt those conversations weren't sinking in with Diamond.

"On Oct. 4th I got an e-mail from somebody who said, "I heard through the grapevine the RIAA is going to sue you," said Ken Wirt, the VP of corporate marketing at Diamond and now CEO of Internet music site Riffage.com. "We talked about it internally. "How can that be? (A) We're clean under the law. And (B) it would make it like David versus Goliath. It would be great for us and probably bad for them."

The law Wirt cited was the Audio Home Recording Act of 1992. Under its terms, the manufacturers, importers and distributors of digital audio recording devices received a limited immunity from liability for copyright infringement.

In exchange, they were required to incorporate into their devices a Serial Copyright Management System (SCMS) to prevent the unauthorized making of second generation copies. They were also subject to a two percent surcharge on sales of digital audio tape and other digital recording conveyances, and required to pay a three percent tax on blank digital tape, discs, and cartridges to fund a royalty pool intended to partially compensate the artists, composers, musicians, publishers and record companies whose works would be allegedly affected by the digital medium.

The law codified specific directions that had long been the Holy Grail of the recording industry, finally granting it a way to slow down and receive a toll from those traveling the digital path. And the RIAA was determined that MP3 recording devices would be governed by that law.

Diamond was aware of its obligations to the recording industry. But Diamond claimed it had no digital output that would make Rio a "recording device," a key distinction under the Audio Home Recording Act of 1992. Thus, it had no serial copy management in its original version.

"The Rio PMP300 portable music player is a playback-only device, and does not record," said Wirt. "Rio simply holds audio content that is already stored on a computer's hard disk and plays back that content."

(Although Diamond did not have a Serial Copy Management System on its device when originally announced in Sept. 1998, by its Nov. 1998 shipping date it had adopted a form of one to satisfy opponents.

In this hybrid form of SCMS, the software on the PC would look at the MP3 file for what's known as a "generational tag," which gives its origin. If the file was encoded as an original, or had no tag, it was transferred from the PC to the Rio. If the MP3 file was already a copy, an error message was displayed).

"In practice, we were never able to find an MP3 file that was encoded as a copy," said Wirt. "Most MP3 encoders either mark all files as originals or don't mark them at all. Just part of the grand absurdity of the RIAA lawsuit."

Feeling confident that it had satisfied all requirements of the Audio Home Recording Act of 1992, Diamond dismissed the e-mail warning as gossip.

But two days later, on Oct. 6, the RIAA sent

Diamond a fax and then followed up with a phone call, asking the company to delay the Rio's launch.

We said, "Why would we do that?" said Wirt.

The RIAA had an answer: other consumer electronics manufacturers had agreed to hold off on releasing similar products, presumably until the recording industry could get its act together.

The RIAA declined to say who the other companies were and how long the delay would be. And Diamond felt that the holiday shopping market would be lost with any appreciable delay in shipping the Rio.

"That's pretty expensive dues to pay to get into a club where we don't know who the members are or what we're going to get out of it," Wirt said, reflecting on the decision to turn down any delays.

The RIAA thought otherwise.

In papers filed in the District Court of California on Oct. 8, 1998, the RIAA and a co-complainant, the little-known and less influential Alliance of Artists and Recording Companies, accused Diamond of creating a portable device that violated the Audio Home Recording Act of 1992, which expressly forbids devices that could make multiple copies of sound recordings. The International Federation of Phonographic Industries and the British Phonographic Industries quickly lined up behind the RIAA.

MP3 recording devices were governed by that law, the RIAA contended in its legal papers. "The Rio does not comply with the AHRA because it is not registered with the copyright office. It does not pay royalties. And it does not incorporate SCMS, which prevents serial copying."

The MP3 community immediately rose up to defend its honor.

Michael Robertson was, of course, at the forefront. The RIAA was "out to do everything they can to squash MP3," he wrote in his "Michael's Minute" column on his

MP3.com site. "It has no intention of working with the (digital music) industry. In business, you don't send a fax on Wednesday and file a lawsuit on Thursday if you want to have a meaningful and productive partnership with a company."

The RIAA was "trying to stall MP3," echoed Ken Wirt.

Instead, the exact opposite happened.

"My analogy is we announced the product and after that there were three people sitting around a campfire in the wilderness trying to stay warm," said Wirt. "It was us and MP3.com and GoodNoise (another digital music net site). And then the lawsuit...it was like they drove by with a gasoline tanker truck and dumped it on our little camp-fire and whooosh! Every major TV network covered it on the evening news, every major newspaper covered it mul-tiple times. I mean, it was like $30 million worth of pub-licity."

Most of that publicity centered on the small guys being slapped by the big bad record industry. Pushing aside the piracy issue, the media for the first time concen-trated on the legitimate businesses on the Net that relied on music licensed mostly from unknown artists. It was easy to draw the line between their right to distribution and the record industry's alleged attempts to bully the lit-tle guys.

Perhaps that notion could be dismissed as paranoia, were it not for something curious that happened around the Diamond/RIAA clash.

In September, 1998, Platinum Entertainment, a large independent record company, was gearing up to announce plans to release free digital downloads of Taylor Dayne, Dionne Warwick, and The Band with Eric Clapton via MP3.com. Naturally, word of that scheme traveled quickly through the gossip-oriented record industry.

"While other record labels may still regard MP3 as a

controversial format, we see it as a powerful promotional tool," said Steve Devick, president and CEO of Platinum, in the release announcing his company's plans. "We intend to drive a large and active audience to both traditional and online retail record stores to purchase our music."

That plan didn't sit well with certain elements.

"We did get a call or two from other major labels that said that perhaps I should re-think my position," said Devick, recalling the moment. "Although I was certain that my position was correct, that it would be beneficial for music sales."

Devick was given a message. No aid and comfort to the enemy camp.

"I think that they thought that we should all stick together on this kind of thing," said Devick. "I'd rather not quote who I did talk to, but the fact is that we heard from a variety of persons that weren't happy with the position that we took. I don't think it was because of MP3.com. That wasn't even a big company then. It was because they thought that we should all have the same attitude relative to the Internet."

*   *   *

Diamond itself pointed out on its web site that it was legal to make MP3 copies of your own CDs, but illegal to code MP3s and distribute them to others unless you have permission from the copyright holder of the music, as is the case with cassette copies of CDs.

But Diamond was doing more than writing. The company also filed counterclaims for violations of state and federal antitrust laws and unlawful business practices under California law, asking for treble and punitive damages for intentional misconduct aimed at injuring the company.

They claimed that the lawsuit was a conspiracy to restrain trade and restrict competition among manufacturers in portable MP3 devices, stopping the legitimate MP3 market.

The first battle took place in mid-October in the Los Angeles courtroom of U.S. District Court Judge Audrey B. Collins. The RIAA sought a temporary restraining order halting any plans to ship the Rio.

As both sides stated their positions, it became clear to courtroom observers that Collins was having difficulty sorting out the complexities of the Audio Home Recording Act of 1992. Like many people of a certain age, Collins seemed to go into a funk whenever the word "computer" was inserted into a statement.

But at the end of the hearing, one speaker rose out of the soupy legalese to help Collins boil down the key issues at stake in the lawsuit.

Attorney Bob Kohn, a cofounder of the GoodNoise MP3 digital distribution site and an authority on licensing, having co-written a highly regarded book on the topic with his father, had filed a declaration and was permitted to address the judge.

Kohn clearly was fearless about the possible consequences of speaking out against the established record industry. He was one of the few who had stepped forward.

"There were a lot of people who backed out of filing a declaration on behalf of Diamond because they were afraid of the wrath of the RIAA," he said later, reflecting back on the trial. "My declaration got longer and longer because I had to testify to more things that other people weren't willing to say on the record."

Kohn's declaration in support of Diamond minced no words, calling the RIAA's battle against the Rio a "smear campaign," and said that their principle argument "appears to be that improved playback convenience of music contained in computer audio files jeopardizes the recording industry."

The lawsuit was not about piracy, Kohn said in his

declaration. Rather, the suit was about control.

"The RIAA is representing the interests of only their largest members in an attempt to maintain control over music distribution and restrict the ability of musicians and songwriters to release their music through distribution channels that are not controlled by the major record companies," Kohn wrote.

Rising in the courtroom that October morning, Kohn was granted permission to speak despite objections by the RIAA.

Basing his case on history, Kohn told the judge that the Audio Home Recording Act was a compromise among three groups: consumers, the computer industry, and the recording industry.

"Back in 1992, everyone could predict increased space on hard discs," he said. "Increased bandwidth and faster telecommunications. New compression techniques. But nobody could have predicted the conjunction of these innovations to provide an alternative means of distributing music. And it was just this kind of innovation that the computer industry was concerned about when it entered these negotiations over this law."

The computer industry was concerned that the future would be stifled, Kohn insisted, so they left themselves an out in the drafting of the 1992 law. If music is copied from an object on which computer software resides, it's not covered under the act.

To illustrate his point, Kohn pulled out a Palm Pilot.

"This device could be a future competitor to the Diamond Rio," Kohn told the judge. "This device has computer programs on it. A computer program that runs my appointment calendar. It has an operating system. It has a computer program that has a calculator, an address book, a database. And it's very simple to add the same technology in the Diamond Rio to this device. It's a computer. That's exactly what the bill excluded."

Collins focused on the Palm Pilot, but reminded Kohn that particular device was not at issue in the case.

Kohn agreed, but focused the judge on the implications of such devices.

"Your Honor, everyone's got one of these now," Kohn said. "And within six months to a year, these things are going to be playing music. Are you going to outlaw these too?"

The speech had a noticeable impact. "When he did that, you could feel a shift," said Hal Bringman, MP3.com's publicity head, who was seated in the court room.

Even though Collins admitted she was troubled by some of what Kohn had said, she nonetheless granted the RIAA's request for a temporary stay, imposing a 10-day stop on shipping the devices.

Collins agreed at that juncture that the Rio apparently violated the Audio Home Recording Act. However, she asked the RIAA to post a hefty $500,000 bond to cover any potential damages to Diamond during the stay while she weighed the request for a preliminary injunction.

It was to be the last triumph for the establishment in the case.

*   *   *

While the legal war raged inside the courtroom, an equally frenzied effort was underway in the media.

The RIAA was on a public relations offensive. To bolster its claims of widespread piracy, the organization claimed it had found 80 sites, most U.S.-based, offering 20,000 MP3 files, "99% of it unauthorized," according to RIAA CEO Hilary Rosen.

The widespread availability of Rio would encourage such proliferation of pirated sound files and "threaten legitimate music distribution on the Net," she said. "We sincerely doubt there would be a market for the MP3 recordable devices but for the thousands of illegal songs on the Internet."

Such remarks would come back to haunt her in Diamond's counterclaims. But even worse, from the RIAA's perspective at that moment, was how much they exacerbated the feeling in the media and among observers of the digital music scene that the recording industry was making Internet distribution into a Holy War.

The MP3 community responded to the threats. At last, the digital music movement had a rallying point beyond a nebulous "us versus them" scenario.

"There is no abbreviation for artists in RIAA," said Michael Robertson, in one particularly cutting remark. "The music industry has been sitting on the sidelines. The train has left the station and none of the big labels got on. They're worried because they're not controlling it."

Kohn also jumped in. "This action has nothing to do with the protection of recording artists and everything to do with the protection of the major record companies from legitimate competition," he said.

The battle lines between old school and new school had been clearly drawn. But the traditional record industry still felt they had a slam dunk case.

They would soon learn that the new school was in the house.

In the grand tradition of smaller, less well-armed soldiers attempting to repel a large and powerful army, publicist Hal Bringman and MP3.com were using guerrilla tactics against the big RIAA machine.

"We went to all the courtroom proceedings and talked to the media that was there and made sure they understood both sides," recalled Bringman. "And whenever they would do the call-in press conferences, I'd make sure Michael always knew and I'd get him in on that 800 number. He'd say, "Hey, it's Michael Robertson," and then ask a question or make his statement and always got in on that stuff."

Bringman and his partner, Phil Cohen, had earlier struck one particularly bold blow in the media wars.

The RIAA claimed to have enlisted through its educational "Soundbyting" program several big artists who supported its efforts to stop Internet piracy. One particularly prominent soldier in the cause was Sarah McLachlan, whose popularity was at a high point owing to her smash album and Lilith Fair efforts.

There was one problem with McLaughlin's participation.

"We contacted Sarah's management and Arista and asked them, "Has Sarah signed up for this?" said Bringman. "And they said, "Absolutely not."

Bringman and Cohen worked that denial for all it was worth in the media. They also obtained an RIAA document with suggested quotes for artists and turned on the media to its contents.

The RIAA was not amused. "The reporter from MTV was laughing," recalled Bringman. "She said, "You have no idea how furious the RIAA is. They hate you guys with a passion."

*   *   *

On October 26, 1998, Judge Audrey B. Collins was ready to rule on the RIAA's request for a preliminary injunction that would halt distribution of Diamond Multimedia's Rio portable MP3 recording device while the legal process continued.

Present in Collins' courtroom were several of the key players from the Rio/RIAA battle and the digital music scene in general, among them multimedia consultant and digital music advocate John Parres, MP3.com publicity coordinator Hal Bringman, and GoodNoise cofounder Bob Kohn.

The judge's clerks passed out the decision to the attorneys of both sides. There was a pause as the papers were rapidly turned by the respective counselors.

"We were all trying to read the faces of the attorneys," said Parres. "There wasn't an immediate indication."

The minutes passed like hours as the attorneys quickly scanned the documents, searching for the bottom line. "We weren't getting any signals," Parres said.

Finally, the Rio attorneys turned to Kohn and smiled. The ruling was in favor of Diamond.

There wasn't a loud commotion in the courtroom. But it was official: the digital music revolution had witnessed its first major battle, and the revolutionaries had won.

Although Collins said the Rio was likely to be considered a digital audio recording device and would have to comply with the Audio Home Recording Act, Collins also ruled that requiring it to contain a Serial Copyright Management System was "an exercise in futility," since copies couldn't be made with it. The matter would be investigated by the Secretary of Commerce, a process which could take two years – a lifetime in Internet time.

The Rio manufacturers would also be required to pay royalties, Collins said. But that wasn't the big issue.

By allowing Diamond Multimedia to ship into the U.S. marketplace, Collins was essentially unleashing the genie from the bottle, and everyone involved knew it.

In a last-ditch effort, the RIAA attorneys appealed the judge's ruling, but they knew that the grinding legal process would likely see relief arrive far too late to matter.

Diamond Multimedia was now free to ship, but they weren't through with the case. On December 2, 1998, Diamond filed a nine-count countersuit against the RIAA, blasting back at the trade organization's attempts to paint it as a tool of Internet piracy, attempts which the company claimed damaged its reputation.

     *   *   *

In June, 1999, the Ninth Circuit Court of Appeals in San Francisco extinguished the last hope of the established music industry. The panel ruled 3-0 that the Rio portable music player did not qualify as a "digital audio recording device" and therefore was not subject to the restrictions of the Audio Home Recording Act of 1992.

The court said the Rio's operation was "entirely consistent with the Act's main purpose – the facilitation of personal use. Because the Rio cannot make copies from transmissions or from digital music media such as CDs and tapes, but instead can make copies only from a computer hard drive, it is not a digital audio recording device."

In essence, the panel of judges said that the digital music portable devices, which allowed users to take their music wherever they wished, were perfectly legal.

A new era of convergent devices had clearly emerged. Appeals Court Judge Diarmuid O'Scannlain said in his brief on the matter that "the brave new world of Internet music distribution was built on new technologies that did not mesh perfectly with existing law." The appellate panel also said that the RIAA's "interpretation of the statutory language initially seems plausible, but closer analysis reveals that it is contrary to the (language) and common sense."

The RIAA tried to put a good face on its loss.

"We're obviously disappointed we lost in the Appellate Court," said a statement, attributed to no specific individual, released on June 13, 1999 by the RIAA. "The court appears to have concluded that, despite Congressional intent, the Audio Home Recording Act has limited application in a world of convergent technologies. Fortunately...the technology and music industries have already come together, in voluntary initiatives like the Secure Digital Music Initiative, to create a secure environment in which consumers can access the music they love in new ways."

Diamond, on the other hand, was jubilant. "The ruling opens a host of new opportunities for us," said David Watkins, president of RioPort, Diamond Multimedia's Internet music subsidiary. "We have always believed that the Rio line of devices operated well within the law. The Rio has always been marketed as a playback-only device for the thousands of legitimate music and audio tracks on the Internet."

On August 4, 1999, the RIAA, Diamond and the suit's nearly-invisible third party, the Alliance of Artists and Recording Companies, announced a settlement of the other outstanding issues of the suit. All three dismissed their legal actions and proclaimed a resolution to their differences.

"Today's announcement makes clear that the future of the digital music marketplace will be created in the marketplace itself, enabled by initiatives like SDMI," said RIAA general counsel Cary Sherman.

*   *   *

Some felt like the RIAA had tried to hit Diamond Multimedia over the head with a mallet, but instead had struck themselves in the knee.

"I know that in large organizations that have been around for many, many years, you develop a certain mindset," said Bob Kohn. "Maybe it's simply a self-righteousness that you know how the world's going to operate. If you're in a big company, it's like a large oil tanker that takes a long time to move. And they didn't understand how to deal with it. So they figure they're going to deal with it like they've dealt with everything else, so that the first thing they did was file a lawsuit against this to stop the players, then figure out how to control this."

"Piracy in the digital world will not be solved in courtroom arguments over good devices and bad devices" said Mark Hardie, a Forrester Research analyst extremely active in digital music. "Rios don't pirate music, people do. Sound familiar?"

RIAA CEO Hilary Rosen also had second thoughts. Reflecting back on the suit in October, 1999, she admitted that there were two major mistakes with the Rio lawsuit.

"There's no question that the filing of that lawsuit focused people like a laser onto what the record companies were doing, and what people perceived that the record companies were doing," she said. "And that was a terrible mistake on our part in terms of not laying the groundwork earlier for the industry's perceptions of opportunity and interest and enthusiasm."

The other mistake is a tougher call, she said, "about whether or not it should have been filed." Given the atmosphere of the times, with MP3 piracy seeming to rage out of control, there was a need to bring technology companies and record companies to the table, Rosen said.

"Now, would they have come if we didn't sue? I don't know. Granted, there's some arrogance certainly in the record industry. But there was a lot of arrogance in the technology industry about how the music industry's just going to have to learn the new way."

Rosen claimed the Diamond experience was the bridge to the legitimate marketplace.

Even Ken Wirt, the point-person for Diamond throughout much of the battle, agreed that the suit seemed to better focus the issues of digital music distribution.

"I think they realized that this negative approach was not working, and hence, I think they decided to take the positive move," said Wirt.

That would translate into the uneasy and sometimes contentious alliance of music, technology and affiliated businesses known as the Secure Digital Music Initiative.

*   *   *

As far back as early 1998, the RIAA was laying the groundwork for the Secure Digital Music Initiative in the media.

"There's going to have to be some technological protections against wholesale unauthorized distribution," said Hilary Rosen. "And it has been our hope that those technology companies and service providers whose businesses are expanding because of the uses of the web will understand that they shouldn't be party to killing the goose that's laying the golden eggs here. That if they want artists to keep creating work, they have an incentive to help protect it."

Thus was born the idea for the Secure Digital Music Initiative, the industry's response to the growing threat of Internet piracy.

On the morning of December 15, 1998, the record companies made their move, introducing the Secure Digital Music Initiative, the first positive embrace by the music industry of the inevitable digital future.

Rosen was joined on a platform at the "Blade Runner"-style Sony Music offices in Manhattan by a powerful but uncomfortable-looking collective of the top executives in the worldwide recording business.

Two of them would leave the press conference shortly after reading scripted remarks and well before they could be questioned extensively about their participation in the announcement.

Bob Daly and Terry Semel of Time Warner's Warner Music Group were even wiser. They sent a statement of regret for their absence that could not be cross-examined.

Besides the record companies, a technology Who's Who was also unveiled that day as backers of the initiative. America Online, AT&T, IBM, Lucent Technologies, Matsushita, Microsoft, Real Networks, Sony Corporation and Toshiba were already lined up.

"This is an exciting opportunity for all of us to be here together," said Rosen. "Today, the recording industry is embracing the digital marketplace with new enthusiasm and new optimism."

The story, according to the RIAA, was that "artists and songwriters and musicians and producers and record companies (the latter noticeably placed last in the parade of beneficiaries) are all enthusiastic about the phenomenal pace of technology. We are excited about what the future holds for music in the digital environment. And we are committed to making sure that those changes are positive, both creatively and commercially."

To underscore that this effort was about artist rights, video clips by several artists were played.

The members of Better Than Ezra were up first. Seemingly ignoring the large and vibrant digital music community that already existed, the boys in the band offered up a rosy picture of a plantation where the workers were happy.

Waxing enthusiastic about their two indie albums and their home studio, BTE turned its attention to online music. "That's why today's announcement is so exciting. It enables bands like us to continue to create and innovate. And especially the people behind the technology; it gives them the peace of mind that their hard work will be respected and protected. We applaud the Secure Digital Music Initiative and all that it encompasses and we look forward to everything it will help usher in for everyone who enjoys music."

Other testimonials followed, from Tracy Edmonds, president and CEO of YabYum Records, co-owned with her husband, Kenneth "Babyface" Edmonds, and songwriter Victoria Shaw, who penned for John Michael Montgomery and Garth Brooks, among others.

Shaw in particular turned up the sympathy knobs. "I'm making my third album, which I am going to sell on the web, so I am very excited about the promise and potential of selling music through the Internet," she said. "But I'm also concerned that the Net be developed in a way that protects the artists and songwriters. You know, we all work too hard to have our music lifted in cyber-space without fair compensation. We need to do this fair-ly and equally so everybody wins."

The point was underlined as the house lights went up. "These videos capture the heart of why we are here," Rosen said. "To protect artists' creativity."

Few were buying that assumption, although Rosen insisted, "It's not about the recording industry imposing a standard on new technologies."

The initiative would be open to all commercial com-panies significantly involved in the technologies related to music, the RIAA promised. The plan was to establish and document an open architecture and a specification for protecting digital music. Products and services that con-form to the specification would then be certified as com-pliant.

The forum would be inclusive, the RIAA also promised. Unstated was that an entry fee of $10,000 was required to join the discussion.

There was one other aspect of the so-called "open" system that was not open to debate, one artfully finessed at the press conference – in the future, any portable device playing an illegally-obtained MP3 would be shut down.

"We are not interested in locking up music forever," Rosen said. "We are interested in achieving a reasonable balance between consumer access and protecting artists and commercial rights."

Many observers, particularly those in the media, ini-tially questioned whether the SDMI consortium would ever meet, given the lack of specifics divulged at the December press conference. Others wondered why the record industry had not learned from the mistakes of oth-ers who had attempted similar security measures.

"I'm sure SDMI's going to be good for the record companies," said Ken Wirt, the former head of marketing at Diamond Multimedia, makers of the Rio portable MP3 device, shortly after the December announcement. "The question is, is it going to be good for consumers?"

Wirt, once in charge of Apple's ill-fated development of the Newton, knew what the likely answer to that question was, given his experience with introducing and educating consumers about cumbersome technology.

"You're a consumer and you go on line and you want to buy this song. If people are confused, you know what they're going to do? Nothing. They're going to use MP3 until they figure it out."

The game industry had gone through a similar process, trying to encrypt their product so consumers couldn't pass it around. "And what they found was it was very effective at preventing piracy," said Wirt. "It was also very effective at preventing purchase. The cure was worse than the disease."

*   *   *

The man the record industry hired to solve its MP3 problem was ironically the same man who helped to create it.

Leonardo Chiariglione, a division head at CSELT, Telecom Italia's corporate research center, was known for his previous work with the Moving Picture Experts Group, which established the standards for MP3.

Chiariglione, a grey-haired, intense executive whose frail frame hid a sometimes fierce attitude, saw SDMI as the continuation of the work he had begun with MPEG, one he hoped would not only protect the music industry from the perils of the digital age, but would also serve to guard future media, like movies, that would also be threatened as bandwidth increased.

"I like being involved and being a guide to a lot of good people who are working to create this new world," he said. "This is what satisfies me."

Satisfaction, however, did not come without a great deal of frustration. Chiariglione was also known as a man

not afraid to raise his voice when negotiations over technical specifications got bogged down in debates. The New
York Times said he angered many of the SDMI's members.

Chiariglione denied losing his temper. And one
could believe him, given that he had a highly Zen outlook
on the task facing SDMI.

"There is nothing that is secure," Chiariglione said.
"What is secure today is no longer secure tomorrow. The
people in security are going to have a nice ride in the next
years because of that. Because security, okay, it's taken for
granted today. But tomorrow a hacker kills that, so now
you have to repair and to bring a new generation of security, too."

That patchwork approach didn't instill a lot of initial
confidence. And confidence was what the major recording
companies needed, given the pressures their artists were
exerting as a new world of promotional opportunity beck-
oned.

Some Dubious Motive or Initiative

E ven as the RIAA and the SDMI consortium mar-
shalled its forces, the MP3 phenomenon continued
to gain momentum.

Suddenly, MP3, the compression format previously the province of unknown bands or pirates making illegal copies of CDs by popular artists, was a growing presence in the legitimate digital music marketplace.

Such acts as Grateful Dead offshoot the Other
Ones, Frank Zappa, Jefferson Starship, Kansas, They
Might Be Giants, Morphine, Richard Thompson, George
Clinton, Roger Daltrey, and John Lee Hooker were mak-
ing their Net debuts in MP3.

Most of the activity came from the launch of
GoodNoise (later to be known as EMusic), a site that
licensed MP3 music for sale, largely from unknown
artists. But the Net's influence was starting to reach the
established label level. Such well-known imprints as Sub
Pop, Rykodisc and Dreamworks weighed in with MP3s.

Admittedly, most of the songs available weren't the cream of the record company catalogs, consisting mainly of obscurities or music from developing acts.

Most big companies preferred the secure formats of Liquid Audio and a2b for their toe-dipping experiments. There was still an uneasy feeling in the air regarding MP3, as witnessed by Capitol Records' conduct when the Beastie Boys and Billy Idol attempted to post MP3 songs.

The Beastie Boys, whose Grand Royal label had a manufacturing and distribution deal with EMI through Capitol, had always been particularly active online, selling merchandise and CDs on its own web site well in advance of most artists.

But late in 1998, the group decided to take their online activities a step further. They posted an MP3 of the single "Intergalactic," then escalated matters by putting up five live versions of their songs, allowing fans to download them for free.

Capitol Records stepped in and pointed out that such releases were in violation of their contract, which gives the company the exclusive right to determine the timing of the release of any recorded music from the Beasties. The group, whose "Hello Nasty" was at that time one of the hottest records in the world, insisted that the material stay.

After some back and forth on the matter, Capitol relented. Faced with alienating one of its biggest acts during a crucial promotional period, Capitol allowed the live material a brief window online. Soon, though, they were replaced by non-downloadable RealAudio streams.

The Beasties, although mindful of their contractual obligations, nevertheless lamented the Capitol attitude.

"The record-buying public is more technologically advanced and more involved with the Web than the people at the record labels," Beastie Mike Diamond (aka Mike D) told the Wall Street Journal. "Nobody is going to stop this. It's out there. The kids are using it."

Others in the industry had differing opinions. Kevin Conroy, senior vice president of world-wide marketing for BMG Entertainment, told the Journal that having the Beastie Boys endorse MP3 files is "disappointing. It makes cleaning up the Net that much more difficult."

But the Beastie Boys had a worldwide following and 700,000 albums sold in the first week of the "Hello Nasty" release. Another artist without that clout fared differently.

Billy Idol, whose days of "White Wedding" glory faded in the early '90s, was making a comeback in the Fall of 1998 on producer Glen Ballard's Java Records imprint, also distributed through Capitol.

In December of 1998, Idol made the songs "Sleeping With An Angel" and "Find A Way" available for free download on MP3.com.

Idol positioned the downloads as a Christmas gift to his fans. Other media reports indicated that there were troubles between the singer and his label, and Idol had been told that the album was not going to be released in its incarnation at the time, leading him to present them online as a way to attract attention for a possible new recording home.

Whatever the true story, the album's sales prospects were iffy at best, given Idol's career doldrums. But Capitol, perhaps smarting from its Beastie Boys facedown, didn't appreciate Idol's Christmas generosity, particularly in partnership with industry whipping boy MP3.com.

After ordering the files to be taken down – Idol's exit negotiations were not complete at that point – the label and artist abruptly parted ways.

"They see this as a crack in the dam," Michael Robertson wrote on MP3.com about the incident. "If every artist did this, that would legitimize MP3 and they're doomed."

Idol may not have had the leverage to achieve his goals. But one superstar interested in MP3 was about to spring a surprise on his label.

*   *   *

Although Tom Petty was still a strong seller and decent hitmaker, there was no denying that the bulk of the anticipated audience for his 1999 release "Echo" wasn't frothing at the prospect of a new release.

Thus, his management embarked on a publicity blitz to bolster awareness in advance of the album's release. Interviews, a live Internet broadcast, three "surprise" shows at a small club – and, most importantly, a free download on MP3.com.

It was that last one that caused a lot of trouble.

Petty manager Tony Dimitriades, realizing the problems record companies had with MP3, yet wanting to maximize his client's visibility, assented to posting "Free Girl Now" on MP3.com in February, prior to the release date for "Echo."

He soon found himself on the phone with Russ Thyret, the chairman of Warner Bros. Records.

"How could you do this to me?" Thryet said. "I found out about it sitting in a meeting where we were discussing what we're going to do in this area and I look like an idiot."

Dimitriades apologized and asked if he should take the file down.

"Not yet," said Thyret.

The day after the Petty song file was posted, a notice suddenly appeared on MP3.com, warning that the file would be removed the next day at 9 p.m PST.

By that point, Warner Bros. had obtained enough evidence of the power of MP3. A reported 156,992 downloads of "Free Girl Now" had been taken from the MP3.com site, with an unknown multiple of that spread

134

across cyberspace via e-mail.

Petty's album unexpectedly debuted in the Top 10. And perhaps its success gave rise to the negotiations that would lead one of the biggest stars in the world to MP3.com.

    *   *   *

Around the same time Petty's download appeared, rumors had surfaced that the Recording Industry Association of America had been phoning parties concerning online music activity. One story had Grateful Dead offshoot The Other Ones receiving a particularly heated exchange.

Hilary Rosen, the RIAA CEO, denied the published and rumored stories that the RIAA warned record labels about using MP3 files as a promotional tool.

"There has been an investment in the activist community that somehow we've been trying to sort of stop it," Rosen said. "And we haven't. You know, (Wall Street Journal reporter) Eben Shapiro tried to do this with the Beastie Boys in a story that he was doing. He was convinced that this had happened, that I gotten Capitol to shut this down. It just wasn't true."

(The activist community Rosen refers to was undoubtedly a reference to Michael Robertson, who wrote in his "Michael's Minute" column in October, 1998 that "a reliable source inside Capitol Records says they receive "regular phone calls from Hilary about their entirely legal use of MP3 files.")

In fairness to the RIAA, it's worth noting that record companies often use the trade organization as both friend and foe of the artists, depending on the need of the moment. Many observers suspect that the RIAA sword was brandished at several artists during MP3 disputes in order to shield the label from the inevitable acrimony.

Rosen, commenting on that time period in 1999, denied the allegations by Robertson. "I have been encouraging (record executives) to put stuff out, not to hold stuff back. Because my view has been that you can't combat something with nothing. The thing that the MP3 phenomena has told us is that consumers want music online. I have been very clear all along that the best thing to do is find ways to move this along, not slow this down."

Despite the uncertainty over the phone calls, it was clear in early 1998 that the RIAA was concerned that pirated files were hampering the legitimate market. Despite a rise of 5% in sales by the U.S. record industry in 1998, Rosen claimed then that the growth didn't come from the so-called "active" buyers, ages 16-24.

RIAA general counsel Cary Sherman offered a personal example of that trend. He said his son, a sophomore in college, had stopped buying CDs.

"And everybody in his dorm has stopped buying CDs, and all of my friends who have college-age kids say that all their friends have stopped buying CDs," Sherman said. "They get everything they need off the Internet. Why should they spend $15?"

*   *   *

Alanis Morissette was coming off the massive success of "Jagged Little Pill" when she launched her second album, "Supposed Former Infatuation Junkie." Fighting the shadow of the dreaded sophomore slump for recording artists, Morissette's management went looking for promotional opportunities.

They found MP3.com, a company with money to burn and in need of a big profile boost just a few months before its initial public offering of stock.

The stakes for both sides were enormous. If Morissette could be persuaded to give even one downloadable song to MP3.com, its credibility with the financial world in advance of its IPO would be enormous, and its credibility as the leader of the heretofore underground MP3 movement would be certified.

Originally, Morissette was supposed to give MP3.com a download. But then the record label powers that be got involved.

Morissette's management, Atlas/Third Rail, was upfront with the executives at Maverick and particularly its distributor, Warner Bros., ironically Tom Petty's label.

The deal was positioned by management as "an opportunity" to have MP3.com and Best Buy sponsor the forthcoming tour, an important one for Morissette in that it was hoped the road would bolster sales of "Supposed Former Infatuation Junkie," which lagged at the time when compared to Morissette's first record.

The target audience for that tour was the 15 to 19 year olds that lived in the MP3 world, many of whom had not yet bought the record.

The problem, as it turns out, was not so much the concept but the execution. MP3 was still perceived as the enemy, and MP3.com was its chief enabler. Warner Bros. did not want to do anything that would look like it was helping the MP3 movement.

Maverick, on the other hand, had less at stake. With no real catalog to protect – the chief reason big record labels were wary of MP3 – the label had little to lose and much to gain. If the Morissette promotion went off successfully, the album's sales could be jump-started.

Negotiations went back and forth. Precedent would be set with the Morissette decision.

Finally, the deal was done. Morissette and her management would get tour promotion and shares of stock in MP3.com. The share figures bandied about included reports of options on 436,000 shares (NY Times) and 658,654 shares (Hits magazine) at a reported 33 cents per share.

No details emerged on how soon the Morissette camp could divest itself of that stock. But MP3.com went public on July 21, 1999 at $20, closing the first day of trading above $63.

For its substantial investment in tour support and stock, MP3.com would get one streamed song of a live performance from both Alanis Morissette and Tori Amos, plus the right to post promotional photographs from the forthcoming tour on the web sites.

"Maverick, MP3.com and I approached this with an open mind, which is what I believe is required whenever there is a shift or an evolution in technology or otherwise," said a statement attributed to Morissette and distributed through Maverick. "I am happy to have the opportunity to connect directly with people who listen to my music and I am excited about the unlimited possibilities the Internet has to offer the artistic community."

Although the Maverick release termed it a "win-win situation for everyone concerned," the victory didn't look like much for MP3.com. The songs would not even be housed on the MP3.com site, but would be on separate web sites created for the promotion.

Given the total amount of stock and promotional services Morissette would receive, it was likely the most lucrative deal in recorded music history. And all for two songs that the public would never be able to keep.

"They said they couldn't pay us in the traditional sense," said Scott Welch, Morissette's manager, to the New York Times. "So we took a handshake and the stock. We didn't know what it would be worth, but it didn't hurt that the deal was in all the papers with Alanis's picture next to it."

MP3.com knew it had been hornswoggled. But having called a press conference, they were committed. Michael Robertson and his newly-appointed president/chief operating officer, Robin Richards, stayed up most of the night at the site of the press conference, the Hotel Nikko in Los Angeles, rehearsing their answers to possible questions about the stock offering and the lack of a download. They were expecting to be attacked.

Surprisingly, there was little controversy the next day. News that MP3.com would not get a download, which was ultimately the goal of the promotion, had leaked the day before. Consequently, instead of a celebration, the press conference had the cautious dread more akin to the announcement of a hostile takeover.

MP3.com CEO Robertson said he wasn't disappointed that the songs would be streamed rather than downloadable. "As long as consumers have access to the music, that's all they care about," he said, nervously parrying the question.

Morissette manager Scott Welch acknowledged that record companies were still reluctant to allow fans to keep free music via download.

"I'm not expecting them to immediately jump on the other side of the fence," Welch said. "I'm just trying to move them over a little."

Morissette, who likely made as much money from the deal as she did on her first album and tour combined, did not attend.

After the press conference, Robertson adjourned to his hotel room. He sat, talking out loud to himself, trying positive reinforcement.

"It was a good deal," Robertson said, rocking slightly and repeating himself. "It was a good deal."

       *   *   *

Even if the Morissette pact was not everything that MP3.com could have hoped for, it did seem to stir up the digital music market even further.

At the same time the SDMI coalition was announcing its specifications for portable music devices – which, unfortunately, arrived too late to have any place in the stores for the 1999 holiday sales season – major record labels and big artists were taking bolder steps into the digital music realm than seemed likely even a few months

before, even if it meant breaking ranks with fellow distributors.

Leading the charge into the digital space by the
majors was Universal Music Group, the world's largest
record company. The company announced early in July,
1999 that it would be working with InterTrust Technologies
of Sunnyvale, California, to securely store, sell, and distribute music for portable devices by the 1999 holiday season,
with plans for wider deployment by 2000.

Larry Kenswil, who headed e-commerce at
Universal, told the New York Times that consumer thirst
for digital music was spurring the company forward.
"The demand is there, and demand is being filled now by
independent labels and illegal content," said Kenswil.
"It's crazy for us to not recognize demand and move."

Also getting into the game was Sony Music. A
week after Universal, Sony said it would release singles
for digital downloading via Microsoft's MS Audio 4.0
during the summer.

Sony had earlier sold singles in streaming media,
which can't be retained by the user, on its own "Celestial
Jukebox," a site that offered mostly older songs.

But now, the company was apparently willing to
take a bigger chance. Although they were confining their
selections to baby bands and obscure artists, Sony
promised to release a "material amount" of singles.

Consumers didn't receive much of a break. Singles
would be priced close to what they sell for at retail, Sony
said, a range anywhere from 50 cents to a few dollars.

"Any opportunity for the consumer to purchase
music in the digital world will expand the marketplace as
a whole," said Sony Music technology head Fred Ehrlich,
echoing Universal Music's Kenswil. "There is a demand
for digital music right now."

*　　　　　　　*　　　　　　　*

Artists were also paying attention to what was

going on, and also ratcheting up their Internet action.

Always-controversial Public Enemy rapper Chuck D was particularly outspoken about his situation.

Chuck D had already had a go-around with a record company regarding MP3. His former recording home, Def Jam, objected to his posting tracks from an unreleased Public Enemy album on his www.public-enemy.com site.

The resulting uproar saw Public Enemy leave the label and set up a series of new ventures, some in partnership with other Internet companies.

A longtime advocate of technology, Chuck D also made the rounds of industry conventions, speaking out on taking control of your musical destiny, particularly by using the promotional power of the Internet.

The record industry's attempts to develop a secure digital music system was "not going to stop the people from getting products free through MP3 and other ways," said Chuck D. "It's not going to stop." Free promotional copies that are passed to radio and retail "will be spread among the web and pirated just like it is now, even more so," he insisted.

The biggest barrier for artists wasn't piracy, he said. "The biggest barrier is legal paranoia. The lawyers don't really know how to call it. They don't know if they're embracing a grenade or something that's going to benefit the art that they do control."

The situation was akin to when FM radio first arrived, Chuck D said.

"Everybody was arguing whether this would hurt album sales and it proved otherwise. Although people could have just taped off the radio, they still wanted to possess that particular piece of art within their own jurisdiction."

The traditional recording industry's unease with cyberspace seemed to be reaching a crest at an April 24,

1999 digital music conference sponsored by the National Academy of Recording Arts and Sciences in New York.

The conference, which featured representatives from many of the industry's leading trade organizations – including its main one, the Recording Industry Association of America – showcased the cultural clash between artists clamoring for the perceived increase in money they believed would arrive through digital distribution, and an entrenched music industry bureaucracy attempting to justify its continued existence.

"The music industry won't support Liquid Audio, a2b, or MP3," said recording artist and Internet pioneer Thomas Dolby Robertson, referring to various digital sound compression formats. "They won't cede control. Right now, we have a great system for them, and one that screws the artists."

Robertson's remark drew hearty applause from the crowd, about half of them local artists. In turn, many cat-called, hissed and laughed at statements from music industry panelists who claimed they were protecting artist rights and revenues, cutting short many of their remarks.

Even companies whose background was primarily aligned with the record industry were starting to break ranks.

ARTISTdirect, whose varied businesses included the Ultimate Band List Web site (www.ubl.com), the Kneeling Elephant record company, and a tour-booking agency for such artists as Beck and Pearl Jam, made a major play to shake up the status quo by announcing partnerships with 45 music groups.

Metallica, the Red Hot Chili Peppers, Aerosmith, the Beastie Boys, Tom Petty and the Rolling Stones were among the top acts signing on to set up Internet "stores" offering their own news, merchandise, physical CDs, and, where contracts permitted, digital music.

Besides sharing revenue from sales, ARTISTdirect also granted stock options to its signees, following in the footsteps of MP3.com's deal with Alanis Morissette. The company was expected to bring an initial public offering of its stock in Fall, 1999.

Although the company downplayed the possibility, the move set up ARTISTdirect as a potential competitor to existing record companies when current recording contracts lapsed, giving the artists the option of bypassing the current distribution system.

Marc Geiger, co-founder and head of ARTISTdirect, tried to minimize his impact on future record company dealings. But he did admit "It's a land grab," adding that he hadn't yet seen any prohibitions against his moves in existing record company contracts. "That'll probably be where the battle lines are drawn."

But strangely, the battle lines appeared to be dissolving rather than forming by mid-summer of 1999.

The Digital Revolution

B y the early summer of 1999, agreement on the infrastructure for controlled digital downloading sought by the big record labels via the Secure Digital Music Initiative was well underway.

Thus, there was no longer a need for anyone to make MP3 a bogeyman, although there was still ample frustration inside record companies – at least from some junior executives – about the slow pace of change.

"A lot of us have wanted to support Microsoft and, frankly, MP3," one anonymous executive told Billboard in May, 1999. "But we are not allowed to because of concerns from above. We sure can't continue to stick our head in the sand and rely only on MTV and radio to expose our acts...These technologies are misunderstood by some of the seasoned decision-makers who just don't "get" the Internet."

That foot-dragging was the main topic of the 1999 edition of the digital music industry's main seminar.

Jupiter Communications, sponsor of the annual and influential Plug.In digital music conference, said that music industry players needed to "adopt a less defensive tact, using digital distribution aggressively as a tool to market and sell music. Industry players have been so eager to dampen any momentum MP3 had as a format that the great benefits of digital distribution – including use of MP3 – remain vastly under-exploited," said Mark Mooradian, a senior analyst with the firm.

Mooradian was trying to tell the industry's players that the time for plotting and fretting and stalling had ended. Digital music was inevitable, and they needed to get aboard the train.

Some were already stepping out of the download closet.

Jim Guerinot, manager of the Offspring and head of Time Bomb Records, told the Los Angeles Times, "There were 18 million downloads and we've sold 8 million copies of the new (Offspring) album. If that ratio holds up, I want 36 million downloads so we sell 16 million albums."

The National Association of Recording Merchandisers (NARM), the main trade organization for U.S. retailers and usually a highly-supportive partner of the recording industry, gave a bitter assessment of SDMI's true motives.

In the NARM "Sounding Board" newsletter, the organization reported "a growing number of the 110 SDMI member companies have resigned themselves to the fact that the major labels are proceeding with internal agendas for secure downloadable music independent of SDMI, and that the labels, having spent years researching and testing a format-independent secure architecture, will ultimately bring their findings to bear on the initiative."

In short, NARM's newsletter suggested, the idea that Internet piracy was the reason a legitimate music market hadn't emerged by 1999 wasn't true. In fact, it might be argued that the MP3 movement constituted market research, proving that the demand for online music existed, while the individual labels readied their own proprietary plans.

NARM argued that SDMI was "ultimately proving more valuable as a consensus-building exercise reassuring technology companies that interchangeability means they still have a vested interest in the space than one actually spearheading the music industry's move into the next century. The initiative has also bought the major labels time, cooling the heels of the MP3 hype while giving them a chance to introduce their own solution to the industry."

The NARM note concluded that SDMI was something of a "public appeasement" that ensured the record companies were in line with antitrust laws. "RIAA has always advanced the agenda of the major labels in Washington through application of copyright laws while maintaining antitrust compliance."

The final confirmation was to come. In what some might view as its Vietnam strategy, the record industry was about to declare victory and get out.

*   *   *

It was near 100 degrees in New York in mid-July, 1999, but inside the Marriott Marquis in New York's Times Square, a proclamation even hotter was about to be made.

RIAA chief Hilary Rosen stunned the audience at the Plug.In '99 digital music conference when she admitted that piracy was no longer an industry concern, just months after the RIAA blamed a precipitous drop in sales among those age 16-24 on just that.

"I can't seem to find anybody to stop talking about piracy," said Rosen. "I don't know if anybody has noticed, but I don't talk about it any more. As a practical matter I don't think we are in a pirate marketplace. I think we are in a place where there is a lot of other things to do and talk about and piracy, as it were, is really not a significant concern."

The people talking about it, Rosen said, "are actually sort of the entrepreneurs who can't find anything else bad to say about the majors, so they say all we care about is piracy."

Perhaps mindful that the digital music revolution had forever changed the way artists could approach the market, Rosen then suggested that the contractual relationships between artists and record companies would likely change in the coming years.

"I think it is entirely appropriate, though, to think about long-term artists having the opportunity to have their own promotion, their own marketing, holding their own masters, doing whatever they want to do with their work and having that level of control," she said.

"Contractual relationships are just that, they're sort of payment for services, and payment in the case of the record companies has usually come first. I think that may change, and it's already changing in the indies, and I think it has the potential to change at the majors where there will be more joint ventures with artists, where if you don't want such a big advance, you can worry less about the issue of recoupment or less about the issue of owning masters."

Suddenly, after months of worrying, fretting, and talking of the long-term, plans for digital distribution of music were ready to come flying out of the closet.

Big-name artists that had been held back by the majors, who cited fears of piracy, were now being put online practically wholesale. In the months immediately after Rosen's speech, such prominent artists as Dave Matthews, Sugar Ray, Stone Temple Pilots, and numerous others appeared with digital promotions. As the music industry headed into its crucial fourth quarter, most major releases were accompanied by some form of digital downloads.

With such momentum building, the whole philosophy of music companies seemed to be shifting.

In one stunning deal, independent Zomba Music made its entire back catalog available to online music compiler Musicmakers, including the No. 1 album on the Billboard 200 Top Albums chart (Backstreet Boys' "Millennium") and No. 3 (Britney Spears' "Baby One More Time"), marking the first time that hit songs were available in online compilations while the corresponding hit albums were still available in stores.

Most record companies had previously limited the number of hit singles by top-selling artists sold at retail stores, fearing that the more profitable album sales would drop if consumers could purchase a popular song without buying the entire album. Suddenly, those fears seemed to be fading.

At the same time the majors were flying, the early movers in the digital music field were also reaping success.

Jeff Patterson, who had dropped out of college and gone into personal debt financing the early days of the Internet Underground Music Archive, finally found a partner that matched his ambitions. IUMA was bought by EMusic for $12 million in stock.

Jim Griffin, who had left Geffen Records early in 1998, was now firmly established as one of the gurus of the digital music realm, a strong advocate of streaming music rather than downloading digits or using the old-school model of shipping content contained on plastic discs. Griffin had received a hefty amount of venture capital, and was said to be planning his own music venture.

Larry Miller, who ran a2b Music in its startup days, had taken his executive team to a new rights management firm, Reciprocal, and was finally winning cooperation from the long-elusive majors and retailers. Similarly, Liquid Audio was making new breakthroughs in the major label and online retail space.

CDNow, which had merged with rival N2K to create

the online industry's largest physical goods site, had a controlling interest purchased in the summer of 1999 by Columbia House, a record club and online retailer owned by Time Warner and Sony. Jason Olim, who co-founded CDNow, agreed to serve as CEO of the company's online/retail division.

And Michael Robertson, who founded MP3.com out of a spare bedroom in his home, formed a joint venture with Cox Interactive Media, the multimedia arm of the cable giant, to create and operate music-related web sites. Cox agreed to purchase approximately $45 million in MP3.com stock at a pre-IPO price of $10.76 per share, almost guaranteeing that the offering would be one of the year's biggest on Wall Street.

Jim Griffin mused on the converging worlds of traditional record companies and cyberspace operations.

"The irony was that I was sitting at Geffen records in my new technology department fielding calls from web sites saying, "We love that new Beck record. Could we stream a copy of it on our web site? If we do, a lot more people will know how good it is and want to buy it." And I would call the legal department and they would call (parent company) Universal and the answer would be no. And at the same time I realized we were spending tens of millions of dollars to convince radio stations to stream in better fidelity these same songs."

*   *   *

The buzz at the MP3.com Summit conference in June, 1999 was heady. The revolutionaries had come to party and celebrate the shifting paradigm that they had helped tilt.

But, strangely enough, there were not the same attacks against the establishment emanating from one of its usual sources, Michael Robertson. One month prior to an initial public offering of stock, Robertson and his staff had pulled in their reins.

"We're watching a change in the world of music and we're all part of it," said Robin Richards, the president/CEO of MP3.com, in his introductory remarks. "And that comes with a great responsibility and I know we all shepherd that responsibility properly."

Robertson, on the eve of the biggest moment of his business career, did some fireside reflecting for the assembled crowd of computer geeks, digerati, and entrepreneurs.

He recalled the first MP3 Summit, 14 months previous, a casual affair that drew 300 people. From a pizza and picnic table affair, it had mushroomed into a gathering that was officially a music industry happening.

"We had a management meeting over the weekend," Robertson said. "The MP3 thing – what is making it go?"

What they came up with is that artists finally had hope, Robertson said.

"We've given them the ability after they've created this product to then get it out to the masses. And for customers, what it's actually done is given them freedom to discover product, to discover talent, to make connections that they were unable to make before. All of that doubled out of this democratic, open access to the music marketplace."

That freedom was about to be taken away from them by a subsequent announcement.

*   *   *

On June 28, 1999, the RIAA's Secure Digital Music Initiative announced completion of the first step in creating its vision of a new digital music marketplace.

At a meeting in Los Angeles from June 23-25, more than 100 large companies from the music, consumer electronics, and information technology industries adopted a specification for portable devices for digital music. The announcement met the ambitious timetable announced four months prior at the first SDMI meeting.

"SDMI will enable the future of music and today's announcement signals to consumers that this future is coming quickly," said executive director Leonardo Chiariglione. "This future holds the promise that consumers will have access to vast amounts of exciting new content with a new level of portability."

Jack Lacy, the chairman of SDMI's portable device working group, took it one step further. "The SDMI specification will allow for the development of consumer-friendly systems for delivering digital music to portable devices," he said. "This flexible specification permits the immediate introduction of portable devices that work for consumers today, and offers even more choices in the future."

Of course, neither Lacy nor Chiariglione took pains to emphasize that many felt exactly the opposite would happen by their actions.

The specification adopted by the SDMI consortium provided for a two-phase system, nicknamed, appropriately enough, Phase I and Phase II.

In Phase I, SDMI compliant portable devices would accept music in all current formats, whether protected or unprotected, including MP3 files.

But when Phase II began – a timetable pegged at 18 months from the date of the July, 1999 announcement – consumers would be blocked from using illegal MP3s. The language in the press release, of course, clouded that issue.

The stranger part of the overall announcement was the vast loopholes left in the specifications.

SDMI would allow consumers to continue to electronically "rip" music from compact discs and transfer it to portable digital music devices, as they had been doing.

However, SDMI would only allow four copies of a CD to be created at a time, three of which could be transferred to portable digital music devices.

If additional copies of a CD were desired, SDMI music users could re-insert the CD into a computer equipped with encoding software and again "rip" the digital codes.

The idea, said SDMI chairman Lacy, was merely to slow those who would use PCs as a "filling station," a scenario where an infinite number of portable devices could be hooked up to any PC and presumably make an infinite number of copies from one disc.

Of course, the loopholes were immediately seized upon by the MP3 community. What about the millions of unsecured CDs already on the market? What if no one bothered to upgrade to Phase II? What about possible work-arounds clever hackers could devise? And what if manufacturers just didn't bother with the specifications?

In truth, all of these questions had but one answer: security was a minor roadblock. Ultimately, the record industry had to rely on the overall honesty of its customers in order to retain its dominance in the current market situation. Absent that, a new paradigm of making money from music would have to be adopted.

Mark Hardie, an analyst with Forrester Research in Massachusetts, took a dim view of the likelihood that SDMI proposals would provide a solution.

"I expect there will be vocal opposition to Phase II implementation," he said. "There will be very little product on the market that adheres to Phase II specification. And MP3 as a format is not the choice of the majors and will never be, as evidenced by recent deals between EMI and Liquid Audio, and the partnership between Sony and Microsoft."

The notion of security was also something Hardie took issue with. "Hackers and college kids will tamper with the devices, because that's what hackers and kids do."

Yet, ultimately, there was a sense of inevitability about the whole process, even among the skeptical, like

Hardie. He, too, seemed to imply that the piracy arguments of the past were a smokescreen to buy time while
the major record companies devised their own solutions.

"I think the record companies have increased their
focus on internal efforts and SDMI is only a faint blip at
the outer edges of their radar. In December, 1998, all five
majors were at the SDMI announcement. None of them
were in attendance at the portable player announcement
(in June, 1999). Hmmmm...the devices at the center of last
year's lawsuit and subsequent launch of SDMI didn't
warrant the presence of major record company representatives. Wow!"

*   *   *

John Perry Barlow was one person who was not
comfortable with the shape the world of online music was
starting to assume.

The cofounder of the Electronic Frontier Foundation
and a Grateful Dead associate, Barlow had a long-stand-
ing reputation for digital activism on his side as he took to
the podium at the MP3 Summit '99 for a keynote speech.

His lecture on that day was viewed in some major
label quarters as a quaint notion, already set in amber, of
some bygone era when the online world promised to
bring a new sense of integrity, opportunity, and discovery.

Yet the digital music revolution and other intellectual discourse on the Internet is predicated on the bedrock
beliefs espoused by Barlow in his speech. Those at the
conference attuned to his message considered the speech
the digital music revolution's call to arms.

We reproduce it here with his permission in hopes
that it will inspire the musicians, record executives and
consumers who are shaping the future world of online
music.

*   *   *

"Inasmuch as law is part of the government's ordering of human affairs, we need to take it into account even

153

as technology's supplanting it in many of its purposes. There needs to be a discourse between law and technology, and, at the moment, it looks more like a fist fight, and it may continue to for a while.

I want to begin by invoking the spirit of Thomas Jefferson, who I'm flattered to be compared to, but that's an invidious comparison. But I want to read you something that he said as he was thinking about what became of copyright law in the United States.

He said, "If nature has made any one thing less susceptible than all others of exclusive property, it is the action of the thinking power called an idea, which an individual may exclusively possess as long as he keeps it to himself.

But the moment it is divulged, it forces itself into the possession of everyone, and the receiver cannot dispossess himself of it. Its peculiar character, too, is that no one possess the less, because every other possess the whole of it.

He who receives an idea from me receives instruction himself without lessening mine. He who lights his taper at mine receives light without darkening me, that ideas should spread freely from one to another over the globe, for the moral and mutual instruction of man and improvement of his condition. It seems to have been intuitively and benevolently designed by nature, which He made them, like fire, expansible over all space without lessening their density at any point, and like the air in which we breathe, move, and have our physical being, incapable of confinement or exclusive appropriation. Inventions then, cannot, in nature, be a subject of property."

Now, there is a part of me, a mean, small, bitter part, that would like to throw my fist in the air and spend the time that I have here railing against the music industry, the recording business. But since I think we have come here to bury them, I think it is only fitting and appropriate that we deliver praise where it's due.

As you see, Jefferson and Madison and the other creators of copyright law in the United States were not necessarily great fans of the ownership of ideas. But they also recognized something important, which was that ideas, in order to travel over distances and freely spread, as they could, needed a transport medium. And in the day that those words were written, that transport medium was the same as it had been since Gutenberg, which was the book.

And so what Jefferson and Madison were primarily trying to do in the creation of copyright was not so much to protect the thinker or the artist or the creator, because they knew they would probably, if he or she were any good at it, go on thinking and creating no matter what. It hardly needed strong incentive. But they knew also that there had to be a medium of transport, and that medium of transport had to be legally protected in order to survive and be able to attract capital and funding and energy and at the same time have a reasonable expectation of return on an investment.

This is somewhat different in other countries, but our copyright law – which, by the way, does not, in any way, cause the ownership of ideas themselves, but only the expression of those ideas, and, in fact, if you read the preamble of the copyright act, only covers the changeable expression of those ideas. It was designed, in large part, to protect the institutions of publishing, in which the record industry is one. And obviously, without the good efforts of the record industry, there is a great deal of music that never would have entered any of our lives. They did an incredibly valuable service to all of us during that long period where the only way to get music spread around the world was in the containers that they make, and I'm grateful to them for that.

I'm somewhat less grateful for their insistence on owning what was in those containers in spite of the fact that those containers had essentially been filled by the genius of others. And I am now not at all grateful for their insistence that they still own most of the music in the world. I think that music is the common property of humanity, and I think that to claim otherwise is to subjugate it to a role that I think is far less than it deserves. It is a form of sacrilege.

This does not mean that I don't believe that copyright has some value in cyberspace. I think that it is important for people to be able to assert some control over their own lyrics. But the revolution that we are here helping to launch is about giving that control back to the people who actually create, and not to the bottling plants. Because the bottling plants can now go away. There is a transfer medium in the world that is capable of reproducing anything that the human mind can create, and doing so infinitely and distributing it infinitely at zero cost, and that is the Internet.

I realized seven or eight years ago that given that fact, it was only a matter of time before technology spread sufficiently and accelerated sufficiently to bring us to the state where we are today, where it is genuinely possible to do without record companies.

Unfortunately, the record companies, in their eagerness to survive – and one can hardly blame them. There are a lot of people making their car payments on the idea that they own music. In order for them to survive, they are running into a terrific battle on both the legal and the technological fronts which resembles, to me, in my mind anyway, the war on some drugs. They are increasingly saying that, of course, they can solve this problem. It's simply a matter of enforcement and education. Where have we heard those words before?

And when they say enforcement, they do mean enforcement. I mean, copyright violations for a long time were civil matters – and recently, thanks in large part to the movie industry and the record industry, they've become criminal matters. And it is now possible to be put in jail for what I believe ought to be a natural human right, which is reproducing music.

Now, I think it's also important to note that I'm not suggesting reproducing the works of others and making money from them without seeing that some of that money goes to the creator. I think that's important and I will talk at some greater length about how I think this can happen, even in these peculiar technological conditions.

But I don't think that having that legal authority vested in the record industry and used in the draconian way that they obviously intend to use it – and a short conversation with Hilary Rosen made it perfectly clear that she means business, and expects to see some people in jail, no matter what public sentiment may say – the others of her kind are putting the interests of their industry ahead of what has become acceptable public practice, and they've managed to get Congress to pass laws that they can use to enforce against public practice.

And they're also talking about going into the elementary schools, and it reminds me so much of the DARE program with praying in the elementary schools and teaching fifth graders just how wrong it is to copy music. This is going to work about as well as it has in its previous efforts with certain pharmaceuticals, and, in fact, there is no known parallel. I think that we are dealing with a cultural battle here between the forces of the individual and his or her ability to do with his or her mind as they see fit, whether it be entertaining with music or other things, and it's also a battle about culture and the culture of institutions, particularly industrial institutions and the individuals of the year to come.

I'm not actually a musician. I was a songwriter for the Grateful Dead for 25 years, until they actually died, but I didn't really know how to play a musical instrument. I did okay anyway. But as somebody who creates music, I have always resented the fact that there were many, many others of my kind whose creations were odd enough, or esoteric, or difficult enough that they were either not able to bring those words to the world because the only transport method wouldn't take them seriously unless they could sell 100,000 units, and they weren't in a position to devote themselves to their real work, since they couldn't dare quit their day jobs. So you've got a lot of really, truly, gifted composers and songwriters and musicians out there waiting tables. I don't know what the restaurant industry is going to do as a result of this. But I guess they'll still have actors.

But it has troubled me for a long time and I also felt that personally I would rather have people hear my works than make money from them. Now, I'm not completely without greed. I'm occasionally accused of being such a hippie mystic by the record companies that I don't care about the artist making money. This is not true. Nobody who worked for the increasingly voracious Grateful Dead as long as I did is immune to the inducements of wealth, because wealth inevitably creates the need for more of it.

And so I'm not at all suggesting that we have musicians working for the common good of humanity and for that purpose alone. We just need a different economic model. And the important thing to realize about that economic model is that the one we have at present is based on the material containers in which information is being passed around, and because of the materiality of those containers, they follow economic laws that are essentially the same as the economic laws that govern trade and toasters, or diamonds and cars. That is to say that there's a relationship between scarcity and value. And that is how the market is being regulated.

The market is being regulated so that music is considered a thing and not what it truly is, which is a relationship between the creator and the audience. Music is not a noun. It is a verb. And it is being treated legally and commercially as though it were a noun because of its containers. Now that those containers are going away, we can start to explore the new realities of the information economy, where instead of regulating toward scarcity in order to increase value, we find that in all likelihood, there's exactly the same inverse relationship between familiarity and value. That is, the more widespread something becomes, the more valuable it is. And this is certainly true in music.

I was in Australia a few years ago talking to a bunch of musicians who were very, very proprietary and worried that people would rip off their music. And I said, you know, it seems to me the problem you folks have is that not enough people are ripping off your music. Nobody knows about it. You would do well to be a little less proprietary because maybe somebody would then hear Australian music besides Australians.

And I know that this works from personal experience. I was hoodwinked into this realization more or less by accident. Back in the early '70s, the Grateful Dead noticed that people were coming into our concerts with tape recorders and they had the natural sort of industrial era reaction, which was to say that these people were ripping us off. And we would kick them out.

And furthermore, we knew and they knew that our value was not in what we had done, but what we hadn't done yet. We never played the same concert twice; we never played the same song twice. So their having what had previously come to pass in no way diminished the value of what had not yet come to pass. In fact, they would go out and attend every single concert on a tour because they wanted to hear the next thing that happened.

This, I think, is a much more incentivizing system than one that places all your value in what you have done. Now, there are many – especially copyright – lawyers who disagree with this, though I find it interesting that copyright lawyers do not resort to copyright in their own economic model. In fact, most people who make their livings with their minds in this country and the rest of the world do not use copyright. They are protected by the relationship that they have with their clients or their audience, whether they are lawyers or doctors or architects or musicians or anybody else who makes his living with his mind.

And that relationship, I would suggest, is a far more reliable method of getting paid over the long term. And it has the advantage of keeping you working when you might otherwise be inclined to quit and stack up a huge pile of money that will ruin your children. I mean, one of the problems I have with the continuous extension of the copyright act – aside from the fact that it seems to have a very tight correlation with the lifespan of Steamboat Willie, or Mickey Mouse, as he's more commonly known – is every time that Steamboat Willie starts to go into the public domain, there's a weird thing that happens, which is, the copyright act protection gets extended again.

So now we're talking about significantly long human lifetimes, long enough to not only ruin your children, but your grandchildren. And I don't particularly want to do that to my kids. The question is, how do you get paid? And I think that there are a variety of methods by which this can happen, although a lot of them depend very strongly on the willingness and ability of people to pay you in certain situations and reproduce your work non-commercially in others. Recently, the Grateful Dead decided that we would make our work freely available in MP3 files. They were already there, but there was some concern that this had a conflagratory character to it, that our work would spread like wildfire in a way that would diminish its value. I mean, we're slow to learn, actually. We saw what the taping had done, and nevertheless, we were afraid of MP3. But, well, there's nothing like money to make you stupid.

In any case, after a fair amount of internal wrangling and discussion, we recently came up with a policy which said – and I think it's one that any artist could use – that as long as the music was being distributed without any economic return to distributors or the duplicators, that it should be left alone. The only constraint that we would impose was that it be that it be purely non-commercial and that we were in no way giving up our claim of control over that music by allowing it to be distributed in this fashion. And I think that's a reasonably good solution. That will only add to the number of people that are willing to come to concerts of what's left of the Grateful Dead, and also add to the people who are willing to buy commercial products, which we intend to produce both for ourselves and others.

I mean, soon it will be possible to go to our web site and click on any song from the 30 years that we played and assemble a CD which you would have in the morning. I mean, if you wanted to have a 12-CD set of all the versions of "Dark Star" ever played, and oddly enough, there are people who would, you can get it. And we also have MP3 files available at a very modest cost. And we think that we're going to do pretty well with that model.

The other thing that we're going to do is set up a record company that does the same service for other artists that would never be able to sign with a major label, but do it as their contractor rather than having them do their work as ours. In other words, we want to reverse the flow of the contract so that we become the servant of the artist, rather than the artist being a servant of us. And I think that that's going to be a successful business, for us and the artist.

There are other economic models, including performance, obviously, as was the case with the Grateful Dead, and there are as yet undetermined ways for the artist to get paid. But I don't really worry about that much. I think that we're developing our sense of that economy. And my principle concern is that the record industry is going to somehow come up with a credible standard for digitally bottling music and impose that on us in such fashion so that they're able to lock up this incredible wealth away from fair use and stifle creation by decertifying the garden from which creation takes place.

I never wrote a song that did not borrow heavily from all the music that I ever heard. It is impossible to be a songwriter without also being a plagiarist. And I think since this is the collective work of humankind, this is as it should be. Now, if all of these things are suddenly bottled up and held close by their current so-called owners, this can't happen anymore. And one of the things that you see them trying to do now, since they're out of the bottling business, is to invariably sell wine by the sip. Which makes it pretty expensive for everybody, and makes it hard for it to travel in that Jeffersonian sense, like fire lit from one taper to another.

SDMI, I think, will die a natural death. But I'm not so sanguine about it that I don't think we all have to be vigilant, because they are also going to be using law in addition to technology, and they are reasonably affected. They certainly have enough money to pay lawyers almost to the point of their own extinction. I mean, I talked to the Sports and Entertainment Law Association recently and I said, you know what, fellows – and they were fellows, believe me – I've got good news and bad news for you. The bad news is that you're doomed. The good news is that you're all going to get rich on the way down. And they cheered! Which shouldn't have surprised me.

And this is, I think, true. There's going to be a massive sue-a-thon. You know, what the record companies are going to die of ultimately is their own legal departments trying to stem the inevitable tide of human desire.

But in the meantime, before that has happened, I think that there is – and we at the Electronic Frontier Foundation think that there is – something that can take place that would be a very bad thing, which is their ability to sharply limit fair use, to make it very difficult for you to hear in any non-commercial way a piece of music. That's what they're trying to do, and when you start doing that, inevitably you're talking about freedom of expression and limiting the ability of people to let their expression self-reproduce, and limiting the ability of others to hear those expressions, and getting in the way of the fertility of the eco-system of the mind. We cannot allow this to happen. There is way too much riding on it, and there are a lot more people in the world that will suffer from its consequences than will suffer from the consequences of the death of the recording industry. And somewhat nicer people, I think, by and large. Well, there I go. It's that mean little part.....

I tell you, you cannot own free speech. I just want you to think about it, because you can't. And at the same time, we recognize that there has to be some balancing between the economic and interests of the artists and also their, I think, appropriate right to control their own works.

And so, we are not espousing piracy at all. But we are espousing a greatly expanded, rather than contracted, sense of fair use, because, as we say here, we have the right to hear, speak, learn, sing, think and be heard. And we do. And so should everyone.

It is automatically assumed in certain quarters, institutional quarters, that we are criminals in our desire to spread human creativity further than leave it its closely-held institutional condition. We don't believe we are. And we believe also that technology gives us the personal power to shift time and space, so that our performances and creative acts can actually become interactive, so that the audience and the creator are more tightly bound than we've ever been before. There are many ways to do this, you know, whether it's webcast performances or more interesting things that allow you to significantly alter the mix of the music that comes in.

I mean, one of the things that the Grateful Dead is considering doing, for example, I mean, we have in our vault tapes of almost 3000 shows, and are digitizing them and cleaning them up. I mean, many of these tapes are pretty full of stems and instead of trying to go to the trouble of trying to clean them all up, we're going to try to create an economy in which others do that task for us, or with us, I should say. And perhaps even remix the tapes so that they come up with superior mixes and also, if they want, create new pieces of music out of the old music that we've made. And we will look forward to the interaction that we're going to be able to have with them and they with each other, because music is also, if you think about where it comes from, it's also about community.

You go to Africa, where I've been spending a lot of time in the last couple years, that becomes evident, because nothing takes place there on a community level that is not accompanied by music in some way. Every once in a while, I have one of those weird moments where something very familiar suddenly becomes unfamiliar to me, and I had one a few years ago where I thought, "Why is music fun to listen to?" I mean, it doesn't have anything to do with food or shelter or warmth or sex or any of the usual human drivers. And I think it's because we deeply associate it with the connection that we feel to other human beings, whether it's in dance or simply those sounds that we have in common at the center of our lives.

So I am proud to be here among you today to protect that human connection and to enhance its spread and density. I think that we are at the edge of what will be a very difficult time legally, and what will be a hard time for many people in terms of trying to make certain that music is heard and heard freely, as it should be. I hope you are all brave and patient in this struggle, and I beg you not to give up.

"Because we are going to win."

Index